I0454243

Turn Your Thoughts Into Wealth: Transforming Your Thinking Into Money Magnet And Unleash Abundance with the Power of Your Mind

By

Jose R. Johnson

Turn Your Thoughts Into Wealth

Disclaimer:

The information provided in this work is for general informational purposes only. While every effort has been made to ensure that the information presented is accurate and up-to-date, Jose R. Johnson makes no representations or warranties of any kind, express or implied, about the completeness, accuracy, reliability, suitability, or availability concerning the information, products, services, or related graphics contained in this work for any purpose.

The use of this information is at the reader's own risk. Jose R. Johnson will not be liable for any losses or damages in connection with the use of this work. It is recommended that readers seek professional advice for their specific circumstances.

Any views or opinions represented in this work are personal and belong solely to [Your Name] and do not represent those of people, institutions, or organizations that [Your Name] may or may not be associated with unless explicitly stated.

Jose R. Johnson assumes no responsibility or liability for any errors or omissions in the content of this work. Jose R. Johnson reserves the right to update or change information contained in this work at any time.

Table of contents

INTRODUCTION

Great greetings, individual voyager! Welcome to a trip that transcends pages - an outing into the real focus of your cerebrum, where the seeds of money related flood lie dormant, clutching develop. In the pages that follow, we're leaving on an encounter together - an examination concerning the specialty of changing your cerebrum into a money magnet.

Anytime inquired as to why a couple of individuals appear to effortlessly attract overflow while others stay uninvolved of flourishing? It's everything except a baffling society or a lucky new development; it's the predominance of the mind. This book isn't just about wealth; it's connected to uncovering the mysterious expected inside you.

As we experience through these segments, think about this more than a read; consider it a conversation, a companion as you continued looking for financial level. We'll loosen up the insider facts of positive thinking, make vision sheets that paint your money related destiny, and track down the speculative energy of cautious money inclinations.

This isn't a responsibility of transient riches; it's a guarantee to change. Your mind, the huge power coordinating every one of your decisions, can reshape your money related reality. We ought to isolate deterrents, modify limiting items, and make a mindset that effectively attracts important entryways.

This present time is the best opportunity to embrace another record, one where your mind is the sketcher of your money related universe. Ready to leave on this odyssey? We ought to turn the page and begin the certainly thrilling outing of changing your mind into a money magnet.

Likewise, remember, as we dive into each part, you're following some great people's example. Think about this book a trusted in pal on your undertaking, giving encounters, philosophies, and a warm push when you truly need it most. Together, we ought to open the way to your financial universe and set out on an approach to persisting through flourishing.

Turn Your Thoughts Into Wealth

CHAPTER 1:

Unlocking the Abundance Attitude

Is it safe to say that you are prepared to open the key to monetary flourishing? In "Opening Riches: Dominating Your Cash Outlook for Thriving," perusers will dig into the brain science of abundance and find the systems and propensities that can prompt an existence of overflow. From understanding the influence of positive cash certifications to dominating cash the board for long haul thriving, this article offers a compact and definitive manual for making a mentality of overflow and going with informed monetary choices. Prepare to assume command over your cash and open the way to abundance and achievement.

Individuals with a sound brain research of abundance practice cognizant spending, getting, and living. Understanding the mental variables of abundance is fundamental in investigating the association among outlook and monetary achievement. Research has shown that people with an abundance brain science have specific qualities and propensities that add to their monetary prosperity. These incorporate confidence, obligation, risk-taking, accomplishment, and assurance. They approach deterrents and misfortunes with strength and view providing for others as their very own feature progress. Obligation is a focal issue in both individual and aggregate monetary circumstances. Notwithstanding, people with a solid brain research of abundance oversee obligation carefully and consider it to be an instrument for pushing forward. They center around making an inward feeling of overflow and significance in their monetary lives, making little strides and settling on cognizant decisions every day to create success and financial wellbeing.

Monetary pressure and uneasiness can be conquered through successful methodologies and attitude shifts. Methodologies for monetary versatility and conquering cash related pressure incorporate making a financial plan, laying out monetary objectives, and fostering a reserve funds plan. Care procedures, for example, reflection and profound breathing can lessen monetary tension and develop inner harmony. By rehearsing care, people can become mindful of their viewpoints and feelings encompassing cash, permitting them to pursue more levelheaded and deliberate monetary choices. Moreover, reevaluating negative convictions about cash and embracing a development outlook can assist people with defeating monetary pressure. By zeroing in on valuable open doors for development and gaining from monetary difficulties, people can foster a more sure and enabled relationship with their funds.

Fostering an outlook of overflow includes moving one's viewpoint and embracing a mindset of overflow and appreciation for monetary thriving. To draw in overflow through mentality shifts, people can consolidate the accompanying practices:

1. Practice appreciation: Developing appreciation permits people to zero in on the positive parts of their monetary circumstance, drawing in more overflow into their lives.

2. Picture achievement: By envisioning and envisioning themselves previously accomplishing their monetary objectives, people can make a feeling of overflow and draw in potential open doors for abundance creation.

3. Set clear expectations: Setting clear aims assists people adjust their considerations and activities to their monetary objectives, empowering them to draw in overflow and make the fundamental strides towards monetary flourishing.

4. Embrace positive assertions: Utilizing positive certifications can help reinvent negative convictions about cash and supplant them with engaging considerations, eventually drawing in additional overflow and monetary achievement.

13

By integrating positive cash assertions into their day to day everyday practice, people can reinvent their convictions about riches and draw overflow into their lives. Positive confirmations are integral assets that can assist shift mentality and make a more certain relationship with cash. When rehashed reliably, these confirmations can neutralize negative convictions and supplant them with enabling considerations and convictions about riches. This training empowers people to foster a mentality of overflow and free themselves up to potential open doors for monetary achievement. By avowing proclamations, for example, "I'm meriting abundance" or "Cash streams effectively and easily into my life," people can begin to revamp their psyche mind and conform to success. These mentality movements can significantly affect one's monetary prosperity, permitting them to show their longings and accomplish more prominent monetary overflow.

Understanding key monetary terms and ideas is significant for people to make informed choices about their cash. It permits them to explore the perplexing universe of money and foster successful saving procedures. The following are four significant justifications for why monetary proficiency is fundamental for abundance creation:

1. Strengthening: When people comprehend monetary terms, they gain the information and certainty to assume command over their funds. They can settle on informed decisions about planning, saving, money management, and overseeing obligation.

2. Keeping away from Mix-ups: Monetary education assists people with keeping away from expensive errors. It empowers them to detect savage monetary items, grasp the ramifications of various kinds of advances, and settle on insightful speculation choices.

3. Creating Financial stability: By understanding monetary terms, people can foster compelling saving systems. They can come to informed conclusions about where to put away their cash, how to develop their abundance over the long run, and how to make arrangements for retirement.

4. Long haul Monetary Security: Monetary education furnishes people with the devices to anticipate their future. They can comprehend the significance of building a just-in-case account, overseeing credit astutely, and planning for surprising costs.

Procedures for Saving and Contributing for Abundance

Computerizing reserve funds and enhancing pay sources are fundamental techniques for people looking to create financial wellbeing through saving and effective money management. Via computerizing reserve funds, people can guarantee a predictable and trained way to deal with abundance collection. This takes into consideration long haul abundance development and monetary steadiness. Broadening pay sources is one more key technique, as it furnishes people with various floods of automated revenue. This can remember ventures for stocks, land, or beginning a business. By consolidating these methodologies, people can expand their abundance gathering potential and make areas of strength for a for long haul monetary achievement. Whether it's through investment properties, profit stocks, or a side business, the objective is to create recurring, automated revenue that develops after some time and adds to generally speaking abundance collection.

The Force of Positive Reasoning

In the immense weaving of human experience, there exists a string, unpretentious yet huge, that breezes around way through the stories of those have achieved money related flood. This string is the impact of positive thinking — an interesting power that transcends the limits of straightforward cheerfulness and transforms into a stimulus for changing the mind into a money magnet.

Here around 10 centers that can help you with practicing the power of positive thinking:

1.The Start of Financial Mindset

At the center of overflow creation lies the start of a financial mindset. The start of money related viewpoint sets out on a trip to uncover the groundworks of positive dissuading respects to overflow interest. It researches how one's mental scene, when created with energy, clears a path for an alluring draw toward financial entryways.

2.The Neuroscience of Prosperous Considerations

Diving into the neurological area, empties the multi-layered dance between the psyche and positive considerations. The frontal cortex, the conflict room of our exercises, answers energy with a troupe of biochemical reactions. The genuine viability of positive reasoning during the time spent making abundance is clarified by grasping the neuroscience behind prosperous contemplations.

3. Framing Overflow Genuine elements

Positive thinking is certainly not a uninvolved onlooker there of psyche of wealth; It effectively impacts the acknowledgment of monetary objectives. The point investigates through the tremendous impact of fostering an inspiring viewpoint, changing cravings into undeniable financial accomplishment. It's connected to causing a mental situation where flood isn't just a yearning yet an ordinary outcome.

4. Exploring the Pessimism Predisposition:
The human psyche much of the time faces a cynicism inclination — an inborn propensity to zero in on bad upgrades — in any event, while endeavoring to accomplish monetary goals. Here it transforms into an assistant, offering

frameworks to investigate this inclination successfully. From seeing and reconsidering pessimistic considerations to developing adaptability, this part plans individuals to vanquish mental hindrances en route to overflow.

5. Attempting Motivation

Speculation meets application in the point, where positive thinking progresses into practical laying out monetary solidness works out. Regular affirmations, portrayal strategies, and mind practices become gadgets in the ownership of those hoping to arrange energy into their money related trip. Genuine models demonstrate the way that these practices can change standpoint into cash.

6.Triumph over Trouble

The outing to overflow isn't protected to difficulties, yet certain thinking fills in as a coordinating light through setback. The point shares accounts of prevail upon money related hardships, showing the way that an uplifting perspective can be the adaptability expected to weather patterns storms and emerge more grounded on the contrary side.

7. Social Overflow Components

Positive thinking loosens up past individual pursuits — it plagues social associations, empowering joint endeavors and important entryways. uncovers how these connections become conductors for monetary overflow and examines the elements associated with developing positive associations and organizations. It's connected to making a climate where total energy upgrades individual undertakings.

8. The Progressively extending effect on Overflow Creation

The impact of positive thinking loosens up quite far past individual overflow creation. Explores the continuously growing impact of positive money related points of view toward a greater scale, influencing networks and social plans. From spearheading endeavors to unselfish drives, find how total energy transforms into a power for uncommon change.

9. Prosperity and Overflow Speculative magnetism

The association between certain thinking, psychological wellness, and money related flood is explored in . The point dives into the physiological benefits of an inspirational perspective — how it works on mental flourishing as well as adds to genuine prosperity. It's connected to seeing that a sound mind is a rich ground for creating wealth.

10. Supporting the Money Magnet Standpoint

As the trip through certain thinking and overflow interest spreads out, In this point it transforms into a manual for supporting the energy. It offers pieces of information into making a lifestyle that supports motivation and overflow creation. From dealing with oneself practices to steady learning, these inclinations structure the groundwork of a legitimate money magnet mindset.

The Persistent Ensemble of Overflow and Motivation

In this examination concerning the trading of positive thinking and overflow interest, the ensemble of these two parts emerges as a persistent, pleasing sythesis. The power of positive thinking isn't just a passing thought or an eccentric conviction; it is a driving forward through force — a chief getting sorted out the tunes of financial accomplishment. May the reverberation of abundance creation become a characteristic and persistent piece of individuals' lives as they keep on further developing their positive reasoning abilities. The journey to change the mind into a money magnet is definitely not a goal; it's a ceaseless gathering, and the aide is, truly, the power of positive

23

thinking. I wish you a rich, thunderous, and steadily developing monetary orchestra.

Overhauling Your Cash Attitude

With regards to individual accounting, abundance creation goes past knowing monetary systems. The capacity to take advantage of the opportunity and capitalize on monetary open doors frequently relies upon one's attitude towards cash. This can be what rouses an individual to embrace difficulties that might emerge in the present, while zeroing in on the drawn out result of monetary achievement.

Figuring out the Cash Attitude

The manner in which an individual sees cash, their perspectives towards it, and the convictions they hold about abundance assume a urgent part in molding their monetary reality. This peculiarity is normally alluded to as the "cash mentality." It likewise mirrors the convictions an individual has about their capacity to make and support riches.

These convictions are much of the time profoundly imbued in an individual's psyche, impacting their monetary choices, ways of behaving, and results. A pessimistic cash outlook, loaded up with restricting convictions, for example, "cash is scant" or "I won't ever be rich," can thwart an individual's monetary development. On the other side, a positive cash mentality that embraces convictions like overflow, appreciation, and certainty can open ways to boundless open doors.

Embrace the Difficulties of Overhauling Your Cash Mentality

Fortunately an individual's cash outlook isn't fixed, it tends to be changed and reworked for monetary achievement. The excursion starts with mindfulness; consider your convictions about cash and recognize any negative or restricting contemplations that may be keeping you down.

Once mindful of these examples, supplant them with positive assertions. Along these lines, an individual doesn't just hug the difficulties, yet in addition finds a way unmistakable ways to defeat them. Confirmations like "I'm monetarily bountiful" or "I draw in abundance easily" can reshape an individual's subliminal convictions over the long haul.

Quickly jump all over The Opportunity: Commonsense Moves toward Develop a Positive Cash Outlook

- **Appreciation Practice:** Show appreciation for the cash that one as of now has and the open doors it brings. Routinely recognize and value monetary gifts, regardless of how little they might appear.

- **Picture Monetary Objectives:** Make a distinctive mental picture of monetary objectives. Representation can improve an individual's faith in accomplishing their objectives, making them more feasible.

- **Persistent Learning:** Keep awake to-date about standards of cash the board, ventures, and abundance creation. Information engages an individual to pursue informed monetary choices, supporting their certainty and outlook.

- **Remain Encompassed by Energy:** Draw in with individuals who have an uplifting outlook towards cash. Positive energy is infectious and can support an individual's own hopeful convictions.

- **Practice Overflow:** Effectively search for amazing chances to share riches, whether through beneficent gifts, speculations, or supporting others in their monetary excursions. The demonstration of giving supports the confidence in overflow.

An individual's cash mentality can possibly shape their monetary predetermination and jump all over the opportunity with regards to monetary open doors. By recognizing their current convictions, testing pessimism, and taking on a positive and bountiful outlook, an individual can overhaul their cerebrum for monetary achievement. Keep in mind, monetary overflow isn't just about financial riches; it's an all encompassing way to deal with a prosperous and satisfying life. Embrace the influence of a positive cash outlook.

CHAPTER 2:

Perception Strategies for Success

Perception strategies have for some time been utilized as a device for sign, especially with regards to drawing in riches and overflow. The idea driving perception is straightforward: by utilizing your creative mind to picture the things you need to appear in your life, you can successfully prepare your cerebrum to draw in those things into your world.

This is on the grounds that the cerebrum can't recognize genuine and envisioned encounters, so by imagining yourself accomplishing your objectives or obtaining the things you want, you are successfully programming your brain to accept that these things are as of now a piece of your existence.

There are multiple ways you can utilize perception to show riches, and vital to find a strategy turns out best for you. One normal strategy is to make a "dream board," which is a montage of pictures and confirmations that address your objectives and wants. You can make an actual vision board by removing pictures and words from magazines, or you can utilize a web-based instrument to make a computerized rendition. The key is to pick pictures and certifications that are significant to you and that resound with the sensations of overflow and success you need to encounter.

Another representation method is to make a "indication map." This is basically a point by point plan that frames the means you really want to take to accomplish your objectives. It can incorporate a course of events for each step, as the need might arise to take and assets you want to assemble. By making a reasonable guide for progress, you can utilize representation to see yourself doing whatever it may take and gaining ground towards your objectives.

You can likewise involve perception methods in your regular routine to assist with showing abundance. For instance, you could attempt "counterfeit it until you make it" by going about as though you as of now have the things you want. This can include things like talking and pondering your monetary circumstance, regardless of whether it right now mirror your objectives. You can likewise attempt representation practices in which you shut your eyes and envision yourself accomplishing your objectives, or you can utilize directed contemplations that emphasis on drawing in overflow and flourishing.

One more impressive method for involving representation for appearance is to encircle yourself with images of riches and overflow. This can incorporate things like filling your home with plants and blossoms, utilizing beautiful and extravagant enhancements, and showing pictures and certifications that address your objectives. By establishing an actual climate that mirrors your ideal reality, you can utilize representation to additionally build up the conviction that you are as of now encountering overflow and flourishing.

It's memorable's essential that perception is just a single device in the sign cycle, and not an enchanted projectile will in a split second carry your objectives to completion. In any case, by utilizing representation procedures reliably and related to other sign practices, like defining objectives, making a move, and developing a positive mentality, you can fundamentally expand your possibilities drawing in riches and overflow into your life.

Note, representation strategies are an amazing asset for showing riches and overflow. Whether you make a dream board, utilize day to day representation activities, or encircle yourself with images of thriving, the key is to zero in on the sensations of overflow and success you need to encounter, and to utilize your creative mind to envision yourself previously living that reality. With steady practice and a positive outlook, you can successfully prepare your mind to draw in riches and overflow into your life.

Making Your Monetary Vision Board

As the new year starts off, what about another way to deal with accomplishing your monetary objectives and dreams? A dream board could be the ideal thing for you.

A dream board, or a fantasy map, is just an assortment of pictures and words showing what you need to accomplish. You glue the pictures on a banner and put it up where you can take a gander at it frequently. This helps you to remember what you need to achieve, and rouses and inspires you to continue to go with choices that help your objectives and targets.

A cash vision board works similarly. The main contrast is that you center explicitly around your monetary dreams and objectives.

Why a dream board?

Recollect the familiar axiom that words generally can't do a picture justice? That is the principal motivation to do a dream board. Pictures summon feelings, and frequently when you can't track down the words to communicate what you feel, an image can finish the work.

Accomplishing a major objective requires inspiration and motivation, and you are bound to succeed when you can picture that objective. An image of a young lady moving on from college, is undeniably more impressive than recording on paper, "Save for my kids' schooling".

Additionally, it is more straightforward to keep your objectives top of psyche when you see them frequently. At the point when your vision block is stuck on a wall or inside your pantry door, you will see it something like one time each day and be helped to remember the fantasy you are understanding.

Instructions to make a dream board

1. Accumulate your provisions. Please, make an actual vision board - one where you glue pictures and words onto a banner or huge piece of paper. The demonstration of truly reordering assists with getting your expressive energies pumping. You will require paper, scissors, paste and a few old magazines. In the event that you don't have magazines, you can likewise look online for pictures and statements and print them out.

2. Get into the right attitude. Making a dream board is an inventive action, so finding yourself mixed up with an imaginative mood is ideal. You are not drawing up a calculation sheet with numbers and rates; all things being equal, you will step into your fantasies and become amped up for what you believe the future should resemble. In particular, make an arrangement with yourself to allow your creative mind to roam free.

3. Page through your magazines or pictures on the web and select anything you like or that your vibe "talks" to you. There doesn't need to be a justification for it - in the event that you like the picture, detach it or print it out.

4. Whenever you've gone through the entirety of your magazines (or online locales), go through the photos and words once more and select your top choices.

5. Pick a picture or statement to place in the focal point of your board and afterward begin gluing the remainder of your determination around it. The significant thing is to not think excessively - permit your instinct to dominate. A dream board is tied in with dreaming past the real factors of daily existence.

6. At the point when your load up is finished, invest some energy checking out and contemplating each picture, word or expression. Feel the feelings it stirs in you and associate with them. You can likewise converse with your accomplice or a companion through your vision board.

7. Set your vision block where it can help you to remember your fantasies and objectives.

What next?

Put in no time flat before your vision load up each day, associating with the motivating feelings you felt when you made it.

Remember your cash vision board when you ponder and design your funds, let it guide you when you draw up your financial plan and when you settle on what to spend your cash.

For example, in the event that you have an image of a family getting onto a plane on your vision load up, then putting something aside for a vacation with your family ought to plainly be vital for you. An image of an individual snickering cool as a cucumber reminds you to do whatever it takes to manage your obligation so you can quit stressing over it.

With your vision board to direct you, you can embrace another way to deal with cash and monetary wellbeing this year.

Showing Overflow through Perception

We face a daily reality such that the quest for monetary flourishing is a shared objective.

Numerous people try to amass riches and partake in the opportunity it can give.

While difficult work, commitment, and savvy monetary arranging are fundamental parts of creating financial wellbeing, some accept that the influence of creative mind can assume a critical part in showing cash.

In this blog, we will investigate the idea of picturing abundance and what it can decidedly mean for our monetary excursion.

The Force of Representation

Representation is a strong method utilized by fruitful people across different fields to accomplish their objectives.

The rule is basic: by clearly envisioning yourself accomplishing your longings, you improve the probability of accomplishing them.

The thought behind perception is that when you reliably center your psyche around a particular result, it adjusts your considerations, feelings, and activities in a way that draws in that ideal result into your life.
With regards to showing cash, perception can be a strong instrument to assist with molding your monetary reality.

By consistently captivating in perception practices revolved around riches and overflow, you make a psychological plan that directs your activities toward making monetary progress.

The Science Behind Representation

While some might excuse representation as simple living in fantasy land, there is logical proof to help its viability.

Concentrates on in neuroscience have shown that the cerebrum doesn't fundamentally separate among genuine and envisioned encounters.

At the point when you picture yourself carrying on with a monetarily plentiful life, the cerebrum sees it as a genuine encounter, which can create positive feelings and trigger activities to carry that envisioned reality to completion.

Besides, the reticular enacting framework (RAS) in our cerebrum goes about as a channel, assisting us with focusing on data in view of our convictions and objectives.

At the point when you reliably imagine riches and overflow, your RAS begins looking for open doors and assets that line up with those perceptions, improving your consciousness of possible roads for monetary development.

Step by step instructions to Utilize Representation for Showing Cash

1. Lucidity of Wants: Obviously characterize your monetary objectives and wants. Is it true or not that you are going for the gold degree of pay, a specific way of life, or a particular resource? The more exact your representation, the more engaged your brain becomes.

2. Make a Perception Practice: Find a calm space where you can unwind and will not be interfered. Shut your eyes, take full breaths, and envision your optimal monetary situation. Imagine yourself encompassed by riches, monetary security, and overflow. Connect every one of your faculties to make the experience more striking — see, feel, hear, and even smell the sensations related with riches.

3. Consistency is Critical: Make perception a normal practice. Put away opportunity every day, ideally in the first part of the day or before sleep time, to drench yourself in your monetary dreams. Consistency supports the brain associations in your cerebrum, making your representations more powerful over the long haul.

4. Positive Feelings: As you picture riches, center around developing good feelings like appreciation, euphoria, and fervor. Feelings are strong energy intensifiers, and they can heighten the effect of your representations on your psyche mind.

5. Conquering Restricting Convictions: It's essential to distinguish and address any restricting convictions you might have about cash and abundance. These negative convictions can disrupt your perception endeavors. Supplant them with positive attestations that support your capacity to draw in overflow.

6. Make A propelled Move: Representation alone is definitely not an enchanted wand for moment riches. It ought to be supplemented by activity. At the point when you picture your monetary objectives, focus on any enlivened thoughts or valuable open doors that emerge. Follow up on them with certainty and assurance.

By reliably envisioning riches and overflow, you free yourself up to new open doors and potential outcomes that can prompt monetary achievement.

Recollect that representation is only one part of the establishing a strong financial foundation process; it ought to be joined by reliable exertion, brilliant monetary preparation, and a development situated mentality.

Embrace the influence of your creative mind and begin showing cash to make the existence of independence from the rat race and overflow you want.

CHAPTER 3:

Careful Cash Propensities

What's care, and what does it have to do with funds? All things considered, care is giving close consideration to what you're doing, second by second. What's more, that consideration additionally incorporates how we spend our cash. Now and again we do it without really thinking, once in a while for satisfaction — and some of the time it might appear to be there's no great explanation by any stretch of the imagination. Rather than careful spending, we could refer to that as "thoughtless spending."

However, there are better ways of monitoring our cash. Rehearsing careful spending might assist with checking Mastercard obligation, cut back on superfluous costs, and set aside cash. We should investigate a few strategies for careful spending.

What is careful spending?

Careful spending is a focused technique for dealing with our ways of managing money. Having a financial plan is an extraordinary method for overseeing individual budgets however adhering to that spending plan can frequently be troublesome. Nobody likes to be determined what to do — regardless of whether it's simply you telling yourself. We go out with companions, we purchase costly dinners, we buy new garments or show passes ... and afterward the bills come. Afterward, we end up singing that standard, worn out hold back, "I can't comprehend where all my cash went."

That is on the grounds that we weren't spending carefully. At the point when we practice careful spending, we might be more ready to stay away from allurement in light of the fact that our spending choices are made deliberately and with thought — not by some coincidence and eccentricity.

Can we just be real for a minute, your financial balance most likely won't develop itself by some coincidence — except if you score that sweepstakes. You really want an arrangement, a strong strategy to follow. Most abundance the board designs basically center around pay, costs, and reserve funds. You understand what your pay is, and you know the amount you put in your bank account every month without adding some second job. Be that as it may, with regards to burning through cash, do you have any idea the amount you spend, down to the dollar? With careful spending, you may.

The following are 10 hints to assist with further developing your cash the board and put you on the way to careful spending:

1. Put it standing by

A considerable lot of us are at legitimate fault for drive purchasing. We see something you need, and we simply must have it. However, we don't necessarily require more garments or shoes, that new innovation, or that much deserved holiday - in any event, we don't require it at that moment.

The careful methodology sets you in a superior situation to save. One way this works is through making a "purchase list." Open the notes application on your telephone — or simply go outdated and utilize a note pad — and add anything you might want to purchase to the rundown on a moving premise. At the point when you add new things, incorporate the date you added it to your rundown. And afterward organization a holding up period. Permit yourself some time, say 30 days, to check whether you actually need the thing. At the point when the time is up, permit yourself the chance to get it. On the whole, really look at the following couple of things on your rundown: Is the following thing a more prominent fascination? Provided that this is true, which thing could you rather have?

This cycle drives you to consider to what lengths you will go for that next sparkly thing and its significance to you.

2. Consider your spending triggers

When do you spend the most? While you're shopping on the web, or when you're at a physical store? When you're separated from everyone else, or when you're out with companions? Revealing your spending examples could assist you with assuming command over your funds and keep your overspending under control.

The careful methodology asks you to comprehend for what good reason you are spending, and that might be useful to control it. You might understand that you spend more out of fatigue, or when you're holiday, or in light of the fact that you feel that you want to stay aware of your group of friends. Realizing that you overspend in specific circumstances could assist you with controling your spending, or assist you with understanding what spending circumstances you might need to keep away from. One way or the other, it's useful to remain mindful of why and when you spend.

3. Track your spending

Knowing where cash goes could assist you with grasping unnecessary spending. While making buys, track every consumption. Represent each dollar. That will assist you with spotting designs, such as overspending at cafés or motion pictures. A $5 mocha latte may not seem like a lot — yet assuming you get one each day, that is $150 per month!

The careful methodology requests that you know that little costs add up. Following will assist you with understanding the situation completely. Utilize that notes application to make one more rundown for following all that you spend. Or on the other hand download an application made explicitly for cost following.

4 . Use cash

There is something particularly valuable about cash. You can't spend what you don't convey. Having just money available will build your consciousness of your assets. Realizing that you just have $50 cash in your pocket — and that is all there is to it, there's no more — could cause you to consider what you're spending for an evening to remember.

The careful methodology advises us that utilizing just money is the most essential type of cash the executives around. It makes you personally mindful of the amount of you possess to spend, and it could help you pre-think about your buy.

5. Make each dollar work

Utilize a lose financial plan — reserve each dollar you procure and spend for a particular reason. Whether it's for food, utilities, or amusement, ensure that your assets are exactly distributed. That incorporates making sure to place cash into reserve funds or into a just-in-case account.

The careful methodology says that when every dollar's a point of convergence, you will generally focus harder on how you use them. Hold back nothing balance toward the month's end - each dollar acquired ought to either be spent appropriately or be saved, whichever turns out best for your financial plan.

6. Consider leaving a particular charge card for "pocket cash"

Some division makes a difference. At the point when you have moment admittance to all your cash, there could be minimal motivating force to control your spending.

The careful methodology requests that you set up a different ledger and to holds store week by week "pocket cash." On the off chance that you utilize a check card for the record, you'll just spend what the record. (However, ensure that the record doesn't permit overdrafts.)

7. Put forth unambiguous objectives

Assuming that you observe that you are spending a ton on one classification, take a stab at laying out a month to month objective. Perhaps you can lessen your eatery spending this month from $200 to $150. One month from now, check whether you can wreck it to $125. Then $100.

The careful methodology alerts you to adopt a ventured strategy and do whatever it takes not to scale everything back at the same time. Make little strides and make sensible decreases until you track down a blissful equilibrium.

8. Go with more affordable decisions

Deciding to eat out? That is fine, yet you don't necessarily need to pick the most costly choice to partake in an astonishing dinner. A film or play is something very similar around evening time or at a midday early show, however the midday tickets are less expensive. Rather than going out to an eatery with companions, what about a bring-a-dish style potluck evening gathering?

The careful methodology requests that you perceive that the experience matters — and individuals with whom you share that experience. Search for more affordable ways of stilling have a great time and partake in the reserve funds.

9. Decide the hour worth of the thing

For any buy you make, sort out the quantity of hours that you needed to attempt to pay for it. Do the straightforward math: take the thing's expense and separation it by the amount you make each hour. That allows you to dole out an individual worth to buys.

The careful methodology requests that you consider, "What's this value, in my time?" Is the item truly worth the hours you spent acquiring it?

10. Freeze your cards

In a real sense. Freeze them. Half-fill a bowl with water, put your credit card(s) in a zip-shut baggie, put that in the water, then, at that point, freeze it. On the off chance that the sack floats after it's frozen, pour more water over it and set it back in the cooler.

That's what the careful methodology says assuming you truly need the card, you'll set aside some margin to place the bowl in the sink and let it defrost. Assuming you want it sooner, run warm water over it. In any case, the deferral — the thawing out — will assist you with pondering why you want to purchase that thing. The time spent defrosting and refreezing the card could dial you back to the point of adjusting your perspective.

Cultivating a Healthy Relationship with Money

When it comes to money, everyone has complicated relationships. The upbringing you had regarding money and morals as a child and the way you processed this knowledge mentally are the two main influences on how you earn, spend, and handle money. For instance, you might tithe to the church if you value religion. You might also make college savings your top priority if you value education.

This relationship with money lies on a spectrum. There are two extremes to financial insecurity. On the one hand, you might be exceedingly thrifty and worried about how little money you have; on the other hand, you might be reckless. Each of us has a distinct way of processing and organizing financial messages, as well as modeling financial behaviors.

What is a relationship with money? A relationship is the connection between two or more ideas, things, or individuals. You are the one who connects with money in a relationship with it. Your financial thoughts, feelings, and actions.

If you're not sure, consider how you feel about other ideas or things in your life. It helps to consider your relationship with money in addition to your relationship with food, exercise, and employment.

How do you feel about money? What emotions do you feel when the topic of money comes up? When you deal with money, do you have any patterns of recurrent thoughts? What word springs to mind the moment you finish the sentence, "Money is [BLANK]"? Our relationship with money is informed by all of these factors.

What is a Bad Relationship With Money?

Although everyone's definition of an unhealthy relationship with money is different, generally speaking, it occurs when you feel aversion to, helpless over, or repulsed by money. when you experience anxiety, financial shame, or other avoidant feelings because of your relationship with money.

Money Relationship Mistakes

The most common error I see in people trying to improve their money relationship is believing that changing a habit will make things better. I like to think of two statements: "If I earned more, I wouldn't avoid my money," or "If I only stuck to my budget, I would feel good about money."

If we want these adjustments to remain, we need to address our relationship with money. Maintaining a budget can be challenging when contemplating one feels confined and trapped. Making more money is difficult when you have mixed feelings about capitalism. We are reminded by Sonya Renee Taylor that capitalism is not the same as money. Under a capitalist system, a few number of people benefit from the exploitation of labor. Money is a tool, a neutral medium of exchange that has existed for the majority of human history. And when it comes to earning more, think about it as keeping the door open for others behind you. By negotiating for a raise, or raising your fees if you work for yourself, you are leaving the door open for other people to do the same.

Heal Relationship With Money

1. Examine your money story. What are your first experiences with money? How was childhood living in your home? What was the tone around money?

2. Forgive past real or perceived money mistakes. We will inevitably feel ashamed of our financial past if we strive for perfection and cling to our perceived or actual financial transgressions. Rather, the key to moving forward is to accept responsibility for your mistake and forgive yourself.

3. Understand the ins and outs of your money.

Another name for this is "financial literacy." I think there are three "pillars" or constants of financial literacy, even though each person's personal financial situation is unique. The first pillar involves creating a spending plan and knowing your budget; the second is setting aside money for intermediate goals, such as a down payment on a home or new furniture; and the third is making investments in your future by paying off debt, purchasing life insurance, and opening retirement accounts.

4. Analyze your financial anxiety and make a list of the money-related habits or ideas that you currently find unhelpful. When it comes to how you wish to interact with money, you are the expert.

61

5. Swap out negative financial habits or ideas for more positive ones. My purpose is not to advise you on how to manage your finances. Here are some starter questions and suggestions to help you replace unhealthy habits or ideas with healthy ones. Is checking your bank account once a week something you consider to be a good financial habit? How about making "I'm confident enough to understand money." your daily mantra? If you typically get upset when you have to pay your bills, consider saying, "I can afford this."

6. Allow for errors and disappointments. Errors are inevitable when you cultivate a positive relationship with money. Plan for bumps in the road as you mend your relationship with money, instead of punishing yourself.

Developing a solid relationship with cash

Cash assumes a substantially more critical part than simply being a mechanism of trade in our cutting edge world. It has developed into a diverse power that influences economies, cultural designs, and our regular routines. While some accept that cash is the wellspring of all underhanded, it is fundamental to recognize that the affection for cash can prompt adverse results. In this manner, it is important to foster a sound connection with cash to accomplish monetary prosperity and in general joy.

Here are a portion of what to consider on the most proficient method to develop a sound connection with cash:

Grasping your cash attitude

Cash is an imperative part of our lives, and the manner in which we see it can essentially affect our monetary prosperity. Building a solid relationship with cash requires a profound comprehension of our cash mentality. A blend of individual encounters, childhood, and social impacts frequently shapes our convictions, mentalities, and feelings toward cash. People who have encountered neediness during their childhood might foster an outlook that believes cash to be an insignificant asset. Then again, somebody who experienced childhood in a rich family might see cash as an image of progress. By pondering these variables, we can acquire important experiences into our monetary ways of behaving and distinguish improvement regions.

Monetary education

A strong comprehension of monetary ideas is fundamental to lay out a sound connection with cash. It is imperative to be know all about central financial ideas, for example, planning, money management, and obligation the executives, as this information will empower you to settle on informed choices in regards to your funds. By figuring out how to financial plan actually, you can plan and screen your costs, guaranteeing that you have sufficient cash to take care of vital expenses while additionally saving assets for future objectives. Numerous assets are accessible to assist you with working on your monetary proficiency and construct trust in taking care of your funds. From books and online courses to monetary counsels and local area studios, tracking down the right instruments to meet your requirements is basic to fostering a strong monetary establishment.

Laying out clear monetary objectives

Laying out clear and feasible monetary objectives is an essential piece of viable cash the executives. It assists you with remaining focused as well as gives an internal compass and inspiration to your monetary preparation. Your monetary objectives could be present moment or long haul, contingent upon your necessities and conditions. Transient objectives incorporate structure a secret stash, taking care of Mastercard obligations, or putting something aside for a get-away. Whenever you have laid out your objectives, it's vital to routinely screen your advancement. Reconsider and change your objectives as conditions change, like a task advancement or another expansion to your loved ones. With a reasonable and definite monetary arrangement, you can remain focused toward accomplishing your objectives and guarantee monetary steadiness for what's to come.

Making a financial plan

Making a financial plan resembles having a monetary compass that guides you toward your objectives while advancing capable spending. To make a sufficient spending plan, begin by ordering your costs and recognizing needs and needs. Allot your assets appropriately, and make sure to audit and change your spending plan consistently to oblige changes in pay or monetary objectives. This will assist you with keeping up with adaptability in your monetary arrangement.

Obligation the executives

As per different monetary counselors, there are two sorts of obligations: terrible and great. Great obligation is cash acquired for ventures with long haul benefits, normally conveying lower financing costs. It helps assemble resources and further develop your monetary prosperity over the long run. Then again, awful obligation includes acquiring for insignificant things or transient delights, similar to garments or get-aways, frequently with exorbitant loan costs and no enduring worth. It can prompt monetary difficulties in the event that not oversaw admirably. Fundamentally, great obligation adds to your financial development, while terrible obligation will in general be a monetary weight without enduring advantages. It tends to be a huge wellspring of anxiety on your monetary prosperity. Focus on taking care of exorbitant interest obligations while making reliable installments on different commitments. Taking on an essential way to deal with obligation the executives further develops your FICO rating as well as frees you from the weight of exorbitant monetary commitments.

Putting resources into your future

Creating financial stability isn't just about saving; it's likewise about effective money management shrewdly. Investigate venture choices that line up with your gamble resistance and monetary objectives. Expand your ventures to relieve risk and think about looking for guidance from monetary experts for a balanced speculation methodology.

Fostering a solid relationship with cash is a continuous cycle that requires mindfulness, schooling, and deliberate activity. By grasping your cash mentality, embracing monetary proficiency, putting forth clear objectives, and taking on capable monetary propensities, you can explore the intricacies of the cutting edge financial scene with certainty and strength. At last, a decent connection with cash contributes not exclusively to monetary prosperity yet in addition to a really satisfying and significant life.

Careful Spending and Saving Methodologies

Setting aside cash is a pivotal step towards accomplishing monetary dependability and arriving at your drawn out objectives. Notwithstanding, saving money on a limited financial plan can challenge. Fortunately with cautious preparation and savvy procedures, saving in any event, when financial plan is tight is conceivable. In this blog, we will investigate viable procedures for saving money on a limited financial plan. From planning and slicing costs to expanding pay and embracing careful ways of managing money, these down to earth tips will assist you with capitalizing on your restricted assets and construct a reserve funds cradle for what's to come.

1. Make a Reasonable Financial plan

The underpinning of fruitful saving money on a limited spending plan is making a sensible financial plan. Find opportunity to survey your pay and costs, recognizing requirements and needs. Focus on fundamental costs like lodging, utilities, food, and transportation. Search for regions where you can scale back, for example, eating out, diversion, or membership administrations. Distribute a piece of your pay explicitly for reserve funds, regardless of whether it's a modest quantity. Sticking to a spending plan will give an unmistakable guide to dealing with your funds and assist you with distinguishing chances to save.

Making an Investment funds Propensity: Reliable Month to month Saving

Costs appear to be continually on the ascent, setting aside cash reliably can be a difficult errand. Notwithstanding, fostering an investment funds propensity is fundamental for accomplishing monetary security and arriving at long haul objectives. Whether it's structure a backup stash, making arrangements for a fantasy get-away, or putting resources into your future, predictable saving is the way to progress. In this blog, we will investigate viable procedures to assist you with making a reserve funds propensity and set aside cash routinely without feeling overpowered.

Put forth Sensible Monetary Objectives

The underpinning of any effective investment funds propensity is putting forth clear and attainable monetary objectives. Find opportunity to distinguish what you need to achieve with your reserve funds. It very well may be pretty much as basic as building a security net for unforeseen costs or as aggressive as buying a home. No matter what the objective's size, having a clear cut reason will give you the inspiration to remain focused on your investment funds plan.

Comprehend Your Ways of managing money

To set aside cash reliably, it's fundamental to have an exhaustive comprehension of your ways of managing money. Track your costs for a couple of months to distinguish regions where you may overspend. Break down your past monetary exchanges, financial records, and receipts. This exercise will uncover examples and assist you with distinguishing pointless costs that can be controlled, subsequently opening up more cash for investment funds.

Make a Reasonable Spending plan

A spending plan is a useful asset that engages you to assume command over your funds. Begin by working out your all out pay and afterward dispense assets to fundamental costs like lodging, utilities, transportation, and food. Be straightforward with yourself while making the spending plan, guaranteeing it mirrors what is happening. Incorporate a class for investment funds, and treat it as fundamentally important, very much like some other fundamental cost.

Pay Yourself First

One of the best techniques to reliably set aside cash is to pay yourself first. When you accept your pay, promptly move a foreordained sum into your bank account. Consider it on the off chance that you're covering a bill to your future self. This strategy guarantees that your reserve funds objectives are met before you get an opportunity to spend the cash on unnecessary things.

Computerize Your Investment funds

On account of innovation, computerizing your investment funds has never been more straightforward. Via robotizing your reserve funds, you dispense with the gamble of neglecting to save or surrendering to compulsions to spend the cash somewhere else.

Begin Little and Develop Slowly

In the event that saving a critical sum immediately appears to be overwhelming, begin little. Saving even a little level of your pay is superior to not saving by any means. As you become familiar with your financial plan and see your reserve funds develop, challenge yourself to bit by bit build the sum. Steady advancement will fabricate your certainty and support the investment funds propensity.

Assemble a Just-in-case account

Life is brimming with shocks, and surprising costs can emerge all of a sudden. Making a just-in-case account is vital for monetary security. Expect to save three to a half year of everyday costs in a different record that is effectively open. A backup stash will keep you from plunging into long haul reserve funds when life tosses curves your direction.

Be Aware of Drive Spending

Drive spending can be a critical barrier to predictable saving. Train yourself to separate between authentic necessities and silly needs. Prior to making a buy, stop and inquire as to whether it lines up with your monetary objectives. Execute a trusting that huge buys will guarantee they are very much thought about choices, not incautious lavish expenditures.

Decrease Superfluous Costs

Recognize regions where you can scale back costs without undermining your personal satisfaction. Assess your memberships, eating out propensities, and diversion costs. Search for financially savvy choices and be aware of regions where you will generally overspend. Divert the cash saved from these changes into your bank account.

Develop Responsibility and Award Yourself
Share your investment funds objectives with a believed companion or relative who can consider you responsible. Routinely update them on your advancement and look for help when required. Also, praise your accomplishments en route. Indulge yourself when you arrive at reserve funds achievements, however guarantee the prizes line up with your monetary objectives and don't wreck your advancement.

Reliably setting aside cash is a significant propensity that prepares to independence from the rat race and genuine serenity. By putting forth reasonable objectives, understanding your ways of managing money, making a financial plan, paying yourself first, and robotizing your reserve funds, you can foster a predictable reserve funds propensity. Embrace the most common way of beginning little and bit by bit expanding your investment funds, while likewise assembling a just-in-case account to shield against unexpected occasions. Be aware of drive spending and track down ways of decreasing superfluous costs without forfeiting your personal satisfaction. Make sure to impart your excursion to somebody who can consider you responsible and praise your victories en route. With commitment and discipline, you can make an investment funds propensity that shows you the way to monetary security and a more promising time to come.

2. Cut Pointless Costs

Cutting pointless costs is a critical system for saving money on a limited financial plan. Examine your ways of managing money and distinguish unimportant things or administrations that you can kill or lessen. Consider arranging bills, dropping unused memberships, or tracking down practical other options. Search for nothing or minimal expense exercises for diversion and search out deals or limits while looking for basics. By cutting pointless costs, you can let loose more cash to apportion towards your reserve funds.

Making a Financial plan: The Initial Step to Building Your Bank account

Building a solid bank account is a fundamental part of individual budget. It gives a monetary security net, assists you with accomplishing your objectives, and empowers you to explore startling costs or crises effortlessly. Nonetheless, setting aside cash requires discipline and a thoroughly examined plan. One of the essential strides in this cycle is making a spending plan. A spending plan fills in as a guide for your funds, permitting you to follow your pay, costs, and investment funds.

Figuring out Your Pay and Costs

The most important phase in making a spending plan is grasping your pay and costs. Begin by social event all the important data, including your month to month pay from different sources like compensation, independent work, or ventures. Compute your complete month to month pay and have an unmistakable image of the cash you have accessible to dispense towards reserve funds.

Then, track your costs throughout some undefined time frame, in a perfect world a couple of months, to get a precise outline of your ways of managing money. Arrange your costs into various classifications like lodging, transportation, food, amusement, utilities, and obligation reimbursements. This exercise will assist you with distinguishing regions where you might possibly scale back or make acclimations to allot more assets towards reserve funds.

Defining Monetary Objectives

When you have an unmistakable comprehension of your pay and costs, now is the right time to define monetary objectives. Figure out what you need to accomplish with your investment funds. It very well may be building a backup stash, putting something aside for an up front installment on a home, making arrangements for retirement, or subsidizing a fantasy excursion. Defining explicit and quantifiable objectives will give you a reasonable objective to pursue and assist you with remaining spurred.

Designate Your Pay

Considering your objectives, dispense your pay to different classes, including reserve funds. Plan to save a specific level of your pay every month. Monetary specialists frequently suggest saving no less than 20% of your pay, however the genuine sum might change relying upon your singular conditions. Be reasonable with your reserve funds objectives and change your costs in like manner to guarantee you can easily meet your saving targets.

Focus on Saving

Savings is an important aspect to consider when creating a financial plan. Treat your reserve funds as a proper cost, very much like paying rent or utilities. Designate a particular sum towards reserve funds every month and make it a non-debatable responsibility. Consider computerizing your reserve funds by setting up a programmed move from your financial records to your investment account. Along these lines, you guarantee that saving turns into a predictable propensity and you don't pass up saving open doors.

Scaling Back Costs

Audit your cost classifications and recognize regions where you can scale back. Search for optional costs that can be diminished without essentially influencing your way of life. For instance, you can feast out less every now and again, limit superfluous shopping, or track down financially savvy choices for your standard costs. Little changes in your ways of managing money can amount to huge reserve funds over the long haul.

Following and Changing

Making a spending plan is certainly not a one-time action. It requires standard following and changing. Watch out for your costs and investment funds every month. Use planning devices or applications that can assist you with keeping tabs on your development and feature regions where you might overspend. Assuming you find that you reliably surpass your spending plan in specific classifications, reconsider and make fundamental changes. A spending plan is a living report that develops as your monetary circumstance changes.

Building a Rainy day account

As you apportion reserves towargs, focus on building a backup stash. A secret stash is a urgent part of a strong monetary arrangement. It fills in as a cushion to cover unforeseen costs or monetary misfortunes, for example, health related crises, vehicle fixes, or impermanent employment misfortune. Plan to save something like three to a half year of everyday costs in your backup stash.

Look for Proficient Counsel

In the event that you find planning overpowering or need help with making a far reaching plan, think about looking for proficient guidance. Monetary consultants can give significant direction custom-made to your particular monetary circumstance. They can assist you with defining sensible objectives, give procedures to obligation the board, and proposition customized guidance to assist you with building a vigorous investment account.

Making a financial plan is the most important move towards building areas of strength for a record. It assists you with acquiring an unmistakable comprehension of your pay, costs, and monetary objectives. By distributing your pay, focusing on investment funds, scaling back costs, following and changing, and fabricating a secret stash, you can lay out a strong starting point for your monetary future. Keep in mind, planning requires discipline and responsibility, yet the prizes of building a sound investment account are certainly worth the work.

3. Expand Pay

Tracking down ways of expanding your pay can give a critical lift to your investment funds endeavors. Investigate valuable open doors for second jobs or seasonal work to enhance your fundamental kind of revenue. Think about utilizing your abilities or side interests to offer independent administrations or make an internet based business. Moreover, search for ways of producing automated revenue, for example, leasing an extra room or selling handcrafted makes on the web. Each extra kind of revenue, regardless of how little, can add to your investment funds.

Step by step instructions to Track Your Reserve funds Progress and Put forth Reasonable Objectives

Setting aside cash is a significant stage towards accomplishing monetary dependability and meeting future monetary objectives. Nonetheless, it's sufficiently not to just bury cash

83

in a bank account; you should likewise keep tabs on your development and put forth sensible objectives to guarantee your reserve funds endeavors are powerful and on target. In this blog, we will investigate useful hints on the most proficient method to follow your reserve funds progress and put forth feasible and reasonable monetary objectives.

Survey What is going on

Prior to defining any investment funds objectives, having a reasonable comprehension of your ongoing monetary situation is fundamental. Begin by ascertaining your absolute pay, including pay, ventures, and any extra wellsprings of income. Then, list every one of your costs, including fixed costs like lease or home loan installments, utilities, and protection, as well as optional spending, for example, feasting out or amusement.

When you have an extensive perspective on your pay and costs, decide your net investment funds by deducting your costs from your pay. This exercise will provide you with an exact image of the amount you can reasonably save every month and assist you with defining fitting investment funds objectives.

Characterize Your Investment funds Objectives

Laying out unambiguous and reasonable investment funds objectives is urgent to keeping up with inspiration and concentration. Your objectives might shift relying upon momentary necessities (e.g., building a secret stash), mid-term goals (e.g., putting something aside for a get-away or home remodel), or long haul monetary yearnings (e.g., retirement or purchasing a home).

While characterizing your investment funds objectives, make them Savvy: Explicit, Quantifiable, Attainable, Applicable, and Time-bound. For instance, rather than a dubious objective like "save for retirement," a Savvy objective would be "contribute Rs. 5,000 every month to a retirement represent the following 25 years."

Use Planning and Reserve funds Applications

In this advanced age, different planning and reserve funds applications can assist you with following your costs, set financial plans, and screen your investment funds progress easily. These applications sync with your ledgers and Mastercards, classify your exchanges, and give significant experiences into your spending designs.

Some famous planning and reserve funds applications in India incorporate Mint, Pecan, and ETMoney. These applications frequently accompany highlights like cost following, objective setting, and reserve funds updates, making it more straightforward to keep steady over your monetary objectives.

Utilize the 50-30-20 Rule

The 50-30-20 rule is a basic and powerful rule for planning and saving. It recommends allotting half of your pay to fundamentals (lease, utilities, food), 30% to optional spending (feasting out, amusement), and 20% to reserve funds and obligation reimbursement.

By observing this guideline, you guarantee that a huge part of your pay goes towards reserve funds, gaining it simpler to follow your headway and accomplish your monetary objectives.

Robotize Your Investment funds
Robotizing your investment funds is a phenomenal method for remaining steady and restrained with your monetary objectives. Most banks in India offer programmed move choices, permitting you to set up repeating moves from your financial records to your bank account on unambiguous dates.

Via robotizing your investment funds, you eliminate the compulsion to spend the cash reserved for your objectives and guarantee that you reliably add to your reserve funds with next to no work.

Survey and Change Your Objectives Routinely

Over time, your financial situation may change because life is dynamic. It's pivotal to consistently audit and change your investment funds objectives to adjust them to your advancing necessities and conditions.

Factors like changes in pay, startling costs, or arriving at a critical achievement ought to provoke a reexamination of your objectives. Be adaptable and ready to adjust on a case by case basis to keep up with consistent advancement towards monetary achievement.

Observe Achievements and Progress

Following your reserve funds progress can now and then feel like a long excursion, particularly on the off chance that your objectives are aggressive. To remain spurred, praise each achievement and headway you make en route.

For example, in the event that you reach 25% of your reserve funds target, indulge yourself with a little prize or enjoy a most loved movement. These little festivals can act as uplifting feedback, keeping you engaged and amped up for accomplishing the following achievement.

Following your reserve funds progress and laying out sensible objectives are fundamental stages on your way to monetary achievement. By understanding your ongoing monetary circumstance, characterizing explicit and reachable objectives, utilizing planning applications, robotizing your investment funds, and routinely exploring and changing your objectives, you can guarantee that your reserve funds endeavors are productive and viable.

Keep in mind, the excursion to monetary soundness is a continuous cycle, and remaining carried out and trained will take care of over the long haul. By making these strides and keeping an uplifting perspective towards your monetary objectives, you'll be well headed to accomplishing the monetary security and opportunity you want. Cheerful saving!

4. Take on Careful Ways of managing money

Careful spending includes being purposeful with your cash and taking into account the worth and need of each buy. Prior to making a buy, inquire as to whether it lines up with your objectives and in the event that there are more financially savvy options accessible. Practice correlation shopping, use coupons or markdown codes, and stay away from drive purchasing. By embracing careful ways of managing money, you can stay away from pointless costs and divert that cash towards your reserve funds.

Step by step instructions to Launch Your Investment funds Excursion: A Novice's Aide

Setting aside cash is a vital stage towards accomplishing monetary security and meeting your future objectives. Be that as it may, beginning a reserve funds excursion can be overpowering, particularly assuming that you're new to the idea. In this amateur's aide, we will furnish you with functional tips and procedures to launch your reserve funds venture. From putting forth objectives to making a spending plan and growing great saving propensities, we will cover fundamental stages to assist you with starting your way towards monetary soundness.

Characterize Your Objectives:

Prior to leaving on your reserve funds venture, characterizing your goals is fundamental. What is it that you need to accomplish? It very well may be building a secret stash, putting something aside for an initial investment on a house, making arrangements for a fantasy get-away, or planning for retirement. Obviously distinguishing your objectives will provide you a feeling of motivation and inspiration to save.

Make a Spending plan:

A spending plan is an amazing asset that assists you with following your pay and costs. Begin by posting every one of your types of revenue and ordering your costs, like lodging, utilities, food, transportation, and amusement. Guarantee that your costs don't surpass your pay. Recognize regions where you can scale back and distribute a piece of your pay towards investment funds.

Set Reasonable Reserve funds Targets:

When you have a spending plan set up, set sensible investment funds targets. Mean to save a particular level of your pay or a proper sum every month. Begin little if vital and steadily increment your reserve funds as you become more agreeable. Make saving a non-debatable piece of your spending plan, regarding it as a cost that should be satisfied.

Computerize Your Reserve funds:

Exploit innovation via computerizing your reserve funds. Set up a programmed move to a different investment account consistently, like month to month or every other week. Via robotizing your reserve funds, you eliminate the compulsion to spend the cash, guaranteeing reliable commitments to your investment funds.

Keep tabs on Your Development:

Screen your reserve funds progress routinely. Utilize a calculation sheet, a planning application, or a committed reserve funds tracker to watch your reserve funds objectives. Keeping tabs on your development keeps you responsible as well as gives a visual portrayal of your achievements, persuading you to remain focused.

Slice Costs and Track down Ways Of saving:
Audit your costs and search for regions where you can scale back. Investigate your optional spending and recognize possible areas of reserve funds. Consider making little way of life

changes, for example, lessening feasting out, utilizing coupons or rebate codes, and tracking down practical other options. Each dollar saved can add to your developing reserve funds.

Assemble a Backup stash:

One of the main investment funds objectives you ought to focus on is building a secret stash. Expect to save something like three to a half year of everyday costs. This asset will give a security net in the event of unforeseen monetary crises, like doctor's visit expenses or employment cutback.

Stay away from Drive Purchasing:
Motivation purchasing can crash your investment funds progress. Prior to making a buy, stop and inquire as to whether it lines up with your objectives. Give yourself a chilling period to stay away from rash choices. Rehearsing careful spending will assist you with pursuing cognizant decisions that line up with your monetary needs.

Look for Ways Of expanding Pay:
Tracking down ways of expanding your pay can speed up your investment funds venture. Investigate second jobs, outsourcing open doors, or utilizing your abilities to produce extra pay. Direct the additional profit towards your reserve funds to help your advancement.

Remain Propelled and Observe Achievements:
Investment funds excursions can be long, so remaining persuaded en route is fundamental. Commend achievements and accomplishments, regardless of how little. Indulge yourself once in a while, yet guarantee the prizes are affordable for you. Keeping yourself roused and perceiving your advancement will assist you with remaining on track and focused on your reserve funds objectives.

Leaving on a reserve funds venture is a significant stage towards monetary security. By following these tips and systems, you can launch your reserve funds venture with certainty. Make sure to lay out clear objectives, make a financial plan, robotize your investment funds, keep tabs on your development, and go with cognizant decisions about spending. With consistency and steadiness, you will fabricate areas of strength for an establishment and accomplish your investment funds objectives. Begin today and assume command over your monetary future.

5. Mechanize Reserve funds

Robotizing your reserve funds is a viable system for reliable and trained saving. Set up programmed moves. Deal with your investment funds like whatever other bill that should be paid. Indeed, even limited quantities accumulate after some time, and mechanizing your investment funds guarantees that you are reliably assembling your investment funds, no matter what your financial plan imperatives.

Instructions to Mechanize Your Investment funds and Arrive at Your Monetary Objectives Quicker

Setting aside cash is an essential part of monetary arranging that permits people to accomplish their monetary objectives and construct a solid future. Nonetheless, it tends to be trying to save reliably in the midst of the requests of day to day existence and the impulse to spend. Luckily, computerization can help. Via computerizing your reserve funds, you can make saving a consistent and easy aspect of your monetary daily schedule, assisting you with arriving at your monetary objectives quicker. In this article, we will investigate compelling techniques on the best way to robotize your reserve funds and speed up your advancement towards monetary outcome On the planet.

Set Up Programmed Moves

One of the least difficult and best ways of mechanizing your investment funds is by setting up programmed moves to your bank account. Most banks in India offer web based financial administrations that permit you to plan repeating moves on a particular date every month. Decide a reasonable sum or level of your pay that you need to in like manner save and set up the exchange. Via robotizing this cycle, a piece of your pay will be consequently moved to your bank account with no work on your part. This guarantees that saving turns into a need and assists you with building your investment funds reliably over the long run.

Use Repeating Stores

In India, banks offer an extraordinary reserve funds instrument called repeating stores (RDs), which are explicitly intended to computerize your reserve funds. RDs permit you to store a proper measure of cash into an assigned record consistently for a foreordained period. The premium acquired on RDs is like fixed stores and can assist your reserve funds with developing. Address your bank and open a RD account with a proper month to month store sum that suits your spending plan and monetary objectives. Via computerizing your investment funds through RDs, you can guarantee ordinary and trained saving towards your monetary objectives.

Investigate Methodical Money growth strategies (Tastes)

Assuming you are hoping to put resources into shared reserves, consider investigating Methodical Money growth strategies (Tastes). Tastes permit you to contribute a decent sum at normal spans, like month to month or quarterly, into a shared asset of your decision. This mechanized speculation approach assists you with tackling the force of compounding and advantage from rupee-cost averaging. Rupee-cost averaging implies that you purchase more units when costs are low and less units when costs are high, coming about in a possibly below price tag. By setting up a Taste with a common asset supplier, you can robotize your speculation and create financial stability after some time.

Amplify Compensation Derivations

One more compelling method for mechanizing your reserve funds in India is by amplifying pay derivations presented by your boss. Numerous businesses give choices like the Representative Fortunate Asset (EPF) and the Public Benefits Plan (NPS) that permit you to contribute a piece of your compensation towards retirement reserve funds. These commitments are deducted from your compensation before charge computations, bringing about potential assessment reserve funds. Talk with your manager's HR division to figure out the accessible choices and add to these plans to mechanize your retirement reserve funds.

Routinely Screen and Change

While robotizing your investment funds is a strong technique, it's critical to consistently screen and change your reserve funds plan. Audit your mechanized reserve funds plan occasionally to guarantee it stays lined up with your ongoing conditions and monetary objectives. Survey your headway, assess your saving propensities, and make any vital changes.

This could incorporate expanding your reserve funds rate as your pay develops or altering your objectives in view of evolving needs. By effectively observing and changing your investment funds plan, you can enhance your monetary excursion and keep focused to arrive at your objectives quicker.

Note, computerizing your reserve funds is a strong system to arrive at your monetary objectives quicker in India. By utilizing programmed moves, repeating stores, precise money growth strategies, pay derivations, computerized wallets, and applications, you can make saving a consistent piece of your monetary daily practice. Routinely checking and changing your investment funds plan guarantees that it stays lined up with your evolving conditions. Via robotizing your reserve funds, you can make ready towards monetary achievement and construct a more promising time to come for yourself On the planet.

6. Search Out People group Assets

While confronting monetary difficulties, it's essential to search out local area assets that can give help. Search for nearby projects that deal support for fundamentals like food, lodging, or utilities. These assets can assist with mitigating a few monetary weights, permitting you to distribute more assets towards investment funds. Also, investigate monetary training studios or advising administrations that can give direction and backing in dealing with your funds.

The most effective method to Track Your Reserve funds Progress and Put forth Sensible Objectives

Setting aside cash is a vital stage towards accomplishing monetary security and meeting future monetary objectives. Nonetheless, it's sufficiently not to just bury cash in an investment account; you should likewise keep tabs on your development and put forth practical objectives to guarantee your reserve funds endeavors are compelling and on target. In this blog, we will investigate reasonable tips on the most proficient method to follow your reserve funds progress and put forth reachable and practical monetary objectives.

Evaluate What is happening

Prior to laying out any investment funds objectives, having a reasonable comprehension of your ongoing monetary situation is fundamental. Begin by ascertaining your absolute pay, including compensation, ventures, and any extra wellsprings of income. Then, list every one of your costs, including fixed costs like lease or home loan installments, utilities, and protection, as well as optional spending, for example, feasting out or amusement.

When you have an exhaustive perspective on your pay and costs, decide your net investment funds by deducting your costs from your pay. This exercise will provide you with an exact image of the amount you can reasonably save every month and assist you with defining proper reserve funds objectives.

Characterize Your Investment funds Objectives

Laying out unambiguous and sensible reserve funds objectives is significant to keeping up with inspiration and concentration. Your objectives might shift relying upon transient requirements (e.g., building a backup stash), mid-term targets (e.g., putting something aside for an excursion or home remodel), or long haul monetary goals (e.g., retirement or purchasing a home).

While characterizing your investment funds objectives, make them Shrewd: Explicit, Quantifiable, Feasible, Important, and Time-bound. For instance, rather than an unclear objective like "save for retirement," a Shrewd objective would be "contribute Rs. 5,000 every month to a retirement represent the following 25 years."

Use Planning and Investment funds Applications

In this computerized age, different planning and reserve funds applications can assist you with following your costs, set financial plans, and screen your investment funds progress easily. These applications sync with your financial balances and Mastercards, sort your exchanges, and give significant bits of knowledge into your spending designs.

Some famous planning and reserve funds applications in India incorporate Mint, Pecan, and ETMoney. These applications frequently accompany highlights like cost following, objective setting, and investment funds updates, making it more straightforward to keep steady over your monetary objectives.

Utilize the 50-30-20 Rule

The 50-30-20 rule is a basic and powerful rule for planning and saving. It recommends assigning half of your pay to basics (lease, utilities, food), 30% to optional spending (feasting out, amusement), and 20% to reserve funds and obligation reimbursement.

By observing this guideline, you guarantee that a critical piece of your pay goes towards reserve funds, gaining it simpler to follow your headway and accomplish your monetary objectives.

Mechanize Your Investment funds

Mechanizing your investment funds is a superb method for remaining predictable and trained with your monetary objectives. Most banks in India offer programmed move choices, permitting you to set up repeating moves from your financial records to your investment account on unambiguous dates.

Via mechanizing your reserve funds, you eliminate the impulse to spend the cash reserved for your objectives and guarantee that you reliably add to your investment funds with no work.

Audit and Change Your Objectives Consistently

Over time, your financial situation may change because life is dynamic. It's significant to routinely audit and change your investment funds objectives to adjust them to your advancing requirements and conditions.

Factors like changes in pay, unforeseen costs, or arriving at a critical achievement ought to provoke a reconsideration of your objectives. Be adaptable and ready to adjust depending on the situation to keep up with consistent advancement towards monetary achievement.

Observe Achievements and Progress

Following your reserve funds progress can in some cases feel like a long excursion, particularly on the off chance that your objectives are aggressive. To remain propelled, praise each achievement and headway you make en route.

For example, on the off chance that you reach 25% of your reserve funds target, indulge yourself with a little prize or enjoy a most loved action. These little festivals can act as encouraging feedback, keeping you engaged and amped up for accomplishing the following achievement.

Following your reserve funds progress and putting forth practical objectives are fundamental stages on your way to monetary achievement. By understanding your ongoing monetary circumstance, characterizing explicit and feasible objectives, utilizing planning applications, robotizing your investment funds, and consistently exploring and changing your objectives, you can guarantee that your reserve funds endeavors are productive and compelling.

Saving money on a strict spending plan might require some innovativeness and discipline, however it is surely conceivable. By making a reasonable financial plan, cutting superfluous costs, boosting your pay, taking on careful ways of managing money, robotizing your investment funds, and using local area assets, you can construct your investment funds in any event, when cash is tight. Each little step counts, and over the long run, your investment funds will develop, giving a feeling of safety and opening up open doors for a more splendid monetary future. Begin carrying out these methodologies today and assume command over your monetary prosperity.

CHAPTER 4:

Confirmations for Monetary Achievement

What are confirmations?
An assertion is a demonstration of affirming something to be valid. It very well may be a composed or verbal explanation that affirms what you need to occur.

An illustration of a nonexclusive certification: I acknowledge 100 percent obligation regarding my own life.

This is a positive certification that emphasizes that you are in charge of your life. The demonstration of rehashing this, either verbally or composed, will assist you with living by it. With regards to cash attestations they are similarly as significant on the grounds that they ingrain convictions that will assist you with making monetary progress. The more you accept your insistences the almost certain you will accomplish the things you set off on a mission to.

Also, the more you consider on something the almost certain you'll be drawn to its chances. This is the reason showing has become so famous on Instagram and Tiktok. Think about this. If you somehow managed to rehash "I generally grin when I see yellow vehicles" multiple times every day for seven days I can ensure what will occur.

You will out of nowhere spot yellow vehicles all the more habitually and begin grinning.

A similar way of thinking is applied to insistences and the pattern of good following good. Notwithstanding, it's critical to take note of that without an inclination toward the activity you'll continuously be restricted. Without making the expected move fundamental you will basically be making statements that have no expectation behind them. Successfully burning through your time.

The most effective method to make your own cash assertions
The hardest part about making assertions is understanding what you need to accomplish through them.

The interaction is significantly more clear once you have a few clear objectives. Cash assertions require particularity, energy, and legit faith in them.

Discover a space to ponder your future objectives. In the event that you're perusing this article there's an opportunity of a lifetime you have a thought of what you're chasing. Perhaps it's a new position, a compensation rise, or progress in business an endeavor. Anything it very well may be ensure you're sure about it.

1. Get clear on what you need

The initial step to making cash insistences is understanding what you need to accomplish. Compose a rundown of the things you need to work out as expected in the short, medium, and long haul. A few instances of this could include:

Increment my reserve funds rate by 20%

A 10% compensation ascend before the year's over

Get three proposals for better positions in your space

Begin putting my cash every month into ETFs and Crypto

Having Shrewd goals is ideal. This implies they're explicit, quantifiable, feasible, pertinent, and time sensitive. Stay away from objectives that aren't in your control.

2. Make a positive rundown of certifications

Cause a rundown of the multitude of positive and negative considerations you to have about every objective you need to materialize. You may be super apprehensive about talking for occupations or terrified of putting away your cash. Ensure you compose all your genuine considerations about every objective. Audit your rundown and change every one of the negative contemplations to the direct inverse. For instance:

Negative: When I interview I get anxious I will mess it up

Positive: I'm sure about interviews and consistently get positive criticism

3. Ensure every one of the certifications are in the current state

This is a key stage in making confirmations. It's significant your attestations are all in the current state. Certifications for the future are less compelling. It's similarly as vital to begin your

115

certifications with "I" or "My". The following are three extraordinary cash assertions:

I'm an extraordinary interviewee

I get more propositions for employment than I want

I deserve a compensation rise this year and I will accomplish it

4. Eliminate every one of the assertions you don't really accept

For your cash assertions to genuinely work you want to put stock in them. In the event that your objectives included getting a compensation rise or saving 10% a greater amount of your cash it wouldn't assist with having totally different and unimportant confirmations.

In the event that your certifications incorporate things like "My total assets is a billion bucks" however you've never begun a business and your friend network is jobless then you're getting yourself positioned for disappointment.

Confirmations aren't wonders, they're a bunch of proclamations you emphasize to yourself to support certainty, assist you with making a move, and spot extraordinary open doors. The most awful thing to do is make confirmations that are up to this point brought you smash your confidence.

So ensure they're authentic, in the event that not, eliminate them.

21 cash certifications to kick you off

1. I'm monetarily certain.

2. I'm monetarily engaged.

3. I deserve monetary achievement.

4. I'm sure about accomplishing riches.

5. Cash streams to me when I want it.

6. My total assets is continuously expanding.

7. I'm appreciative for the cash I make.

8. My relationship with cash is solid.

9. I decide to be rich and effective.

10. I set out my own monetary open doors.

11. My life is topping off with monetary achievement.

12. My business is building me the existence I want.

13. The entryways I open lead to monetary achievement.

14. I can with certainty vanquish my cash objectives.

15. Each dollar I spend returns duplicated.

16. The cash I procure and spend satisfies me.

17. I'm not poor, I'm just structure my fantasy life.

18. I generally have more cash coming in than going out.

19. I'm continuously exploiting valuable open doors that current themselves.

20. I'm purposefully creating financial wellbeing. It is a cycle I appreciate without question.

21. Cash is utilized to give extraordinary things to my life and the existences of my loved ones.

Regardless of whether you're persuaded, there is no drawback to making cash assertions. You lose nothing through doing them. There's proof that demonstrates they can help and the potential gain is more noteworthy than the drawback. So it merits a shot! If you have any desire to begin with something somewhat more straightforward maybe take a stab at journaling.

Making Strong Cash Confirmations

In the event that you're hoping to utilize confirmations to advance your monetary circumstance, there are a couple of things you ought to remember. To start with, it's vital to be explicit while creating your certifications. Dubious explanations like "I'm well off" or "I merit overflow" are probably not going to have a lot of an effect.

All things considered, center around making insistences that address a particular objective or want. For instance, on the off chance that you're expecting to draw in more cash into your life, you could express something like "I'm drawing in expanding measures of cash consistently" or " Consistently, I'm turning out to be all the more monetarily effective."

Having confidence in what you're talking about is additionally significant. Insistences possibly work assuming you really trust them. So on the off chance that you're experiencing difficulty accepting your certifications, have a go at rehashing them to yourself on various occasions over the course of the day, or thinking of them down and perusing them back to yourself consistently.

Assertions to Bring in Cash

In the event that you're hoping to show more cash into your life, utilizing confirmations is an amazing asset that can help. Certifications are positive explanations that you rehash to yourself consistently to program your psyche mind for progress.

Certain individuals accept that basically by rehashing these insistences, they will see an inundation of money. Nonetheless, it's vital to comprehend how the general rule that good energy attracts good works to really utilize attestations.

The pattern of good following good is the conviction that like draws in like. As such, anything that considerations and feelings you center around will be drawn to your life. To this end it's so essential to zero in on good considerations and sentiments to draw in certain encounters into your life.

Here are some strong cash attestations that can assist you with showing more riches and overflow:

1. I'm a cash magnet.

2. Cash comes to me effectively and easily.

3. I genuinely deserve overflow.

4. I'm available to getting all the decency that life brings to the table.

5. I should be rich and effective

I'm appreciative for all the overflow in my life. By zeroing in on these positive assertions, you can program your psyche brain to draw in more cash into your life. Keep in mind, it's essential to zero in on what you need, not what you don't need. In this way, rather than stressing over not having sufficient cash, center around drawing in overflow into your life.

As well as utilizing insistences, there are different things you can do to show more cash. Perception is another incredible asset that can assist you with drawing in riches and overflow. Put shortly every day picturing yourself as the effective, bountiful individual you need to be. See yourself having all the cash you want and carrying on with your fantasy life.

Feel the feelings of bliss, euphoria, and appreciation as though you have proactively accomplished your objectives. The more genuine you can cause it to feel, the better. Likewise, make a move towards your objectives. To bring in more cash, search for ways of expanding your pay or go into business. The pattern of good following good works best when joined with positive activity.How great are confirmations at bringing in cash?

A great many people might want to accept that insistences are a few enchantment words that can mystically draw in cash into our lives. While it is actually the case that confirmations can assist with centering our psyches and change our reasoning examples, they won't work except if we make a move towards our objectives. While there is nobody equation for progress, utilizing confirmations can be a useful device in Showing your fantasies into the real world. Continue to peruse to find a few compelling insistences that can assist you with drawing in more cash into your life.

Certifications are positive articulations that can assist you with testing and defeat negative, behaving destructively convictions. With regards to bringing in cash, certifications can assist you with putting stock in your own capacity to produce pay and manifest abundance. While there is no assurance that utilizing confirmations will prompt quick wealth, they can assist with moving your outlook in a more certain course and open up new open doors for overflow. Confirmations are strong articulations that can assist you with drawing in what you want into your life. With regards to cash, utilizing attestations can assist you with drawing in overflow and flourishing.

There is no rejecting that certifications can be strong. They can assist us with zeroing in on what we need, and help us to remember our objectives when we want to surrender. In any case, in the event that we just depend on attestations without making any move, we are probably going to be frustrated with the outcomes.

Certifications can assist us with zeroing in on what we need, yet they won't work except if we really effectively get it going. For insistences to be successful, we want to uphold them with activity. Really at that time could we at any point hope to see any genuine outcomes.

The Professionals of Attestations in Bringing in Cash

A great many people accept that involving certifications can help people in drawing in and showing cash. According to the pattern of good following good, what we think and feel is what we draw in our lives. Thus, in the event that we continue to think positive contemplations about cash, we are bound to draw in cash into our lives. Insistences work on a similar standard. By rehashing specific cash attestations consistently, we program our psyches to zero in on overflow and achievement, which thus assists us with drawing in more cash.

A portion of the advantages of involving certifications for cash include:

Assisting you with remaining fixed on your objectives: When you continue to rehash your attestations, it assists you with remaining fixed on your objectives. This is on the grounds that each time you say your certifications, you are supporting your craving to accomplish your objectives.

At the point when you continue to rehash your assertions, it assists you with keeping fixed on your objectives. This is on the grounds that each time you say your assertions, you are supporting your longing to accomplish your objectives. Assisting you with disposing of negative convictions: A considerable lot of us have negative convictions about cash that we have gotten from our loved ones. These convictions can keep us from accomplishing our monetary objectives. By utilizing confirmations, we can dispose of these negative convictions and supplant them with positive ones.

A large number of us have negative convictions about cash that we have gotten from our loved ones. These convictions can keep us from accomplishing our monetary objectives. By utilizing assertions, we can dispose of these negative convictions and supplant them with positive ones. Assisting you with drawing in abundance: As referenced prior, confirmations can assist you with drawing in abundance into your life. This is on the grounds that when you continue to think positive considerations about cash, you are bound to draw in cash into your life.

As referenced before, attestations can assist you with drawing in abundance into your life. This is on the grounds that when you continue to think positive contemplations about cash, you are bound to draw in cash into your life. Assisting you with showing your cravings: By utilizing certifications, you can program your psyche to zero in on your longings. This will assist you with showing your longings into the real world.

Assertions for Riches

Insistences can be an extraordinary instrument for showing riches, however they ought to be utilized cautiously and with balance. Remember that cash isn't the main thing that is important throughout everyday life, and don't allow your confirmations to assume control over your viewpoints and activities. With cautious thought and use, notwithstanding, attestations can assist you with drawing in more overflow into your life.

Day to day Attestation Ceremonies for Riches

In the gigantic scene of mindfulness, the possibility of ordinary affirmations stays as a strong gadget, an everyday custom that transcends day to day timetable and transforms into an extraordinary influence in embellishment one's standpoint towards wealth. This preparing isn't straightforward emphasis of positive articulations; it's a deliberate and key exhibit highlighted remaking the mind. We ought to

129

dive straight into the center of regular verification customs for wealth and uncover the momentous impact they utilize.

The Underpinnings of Verifications: Improving the Mind

Demands work on the standard of revamping the mind. The internal brain, like a calm maestro, sorts out the majority of our perspectives, convictions, and approaches to acting. By embedding positive confirmations reliably, individuals can really take a look at limiting convictions and supersede them with drawing in contemplations rotated around wealth and flood.

Making Your Overflow Mantras: Precision and Point

The sufficiency of everyday affirmations lies in their precision and point. Rather than nonexclusive articulations, making express and assigned verifications works on their impact. For overflow creation, affirmations should be custom fitted to address financial goals, attitude developments, and sureness building. It's connected to articulating the best reality with clearness and conviction.

Joining into Everyday Regular practice: Consistency is Crucial

Consistency is the critical piece of confirmation customs. Compromise into regular timetables ensures that these affirmations become a steady piece of one's viewpoint. Whether examined in the initial segment of the day, during breaks, or before rest, the key is to make declarations a natural and non-questionable piece of everyday presence.

Significant Resonation: Lifting Accreditations Past anything describable

Demands should not be basic verbal recitations; they should bring out authentic sentiments. Communicating really with affirmations introduces them significantly into the mind. It's connected to feeling the flood, imagining the overflow, and experiencing the sentiments related with financial accomplishment.

Positive Affirmations for Overflow Creation: Models and Recipes

Affirmations for overflow can take various designs, watching out for different highlights of the overflow standpoint. Models include:

- "I'm a magnet for money related flourishing."
- "Cash streams effectively into my life."
- "I merit wealth and accomplishment."
- "I attract open entryways that lead to money related flood."

Recipes for causing attestations to incorporate using present status, being positive, and avoiding invalidations. For instance, instead of saying, "I'm not submerged," one could declare, "I'm financially free."

Statements in Portrayal Chips away at: Orchestrating Your Financial Picture

Coordinating affirmations with discernment escalates their impact. Make a mental image of the best overflow circumstance while examining confirmations. It's connected to showing accomplishment, embedding it in the mind, and allowing the mind to seek after making that vision a reality.

Tweaking Affirmations: Fitting to Individual Goals

Individualizing accreditations changes them to express financial goals. Whether going all in, commitment lessening, or adventure wins, fitting declarations ensures they resound with individual cravings. Personalization supports a more significant relationship with the certificates, upgrading their unprecedented effect.

Affirmations as a Sureness Ally: Empowering Self-Conviction

Past overflow creation, affirmations go about areas of strength for as allies. By affirming one's capacities, adaptability, and deservingness of wealth, individuals develop self-conviction. This conviction transforms into a central purpose in taking striking financial actions, making the most of possibilities, and investigating challenges with balance.

Certificates in Previews of Challenge: A Defend of Energy

Indeed, even with financial disasters or challenges, confirmations become a protect of energy. Right when weakness looms, affirming adaptability, flexibility, and the sureness of money related recovery upholds a mindset of consistency. It's connected to including affirmations as a sign of light during depictions of money related roughness.

Demands for Flood Past Assets: Thorough Overflow Viewpoint

Ordinary confirmation customs loosen up past monetary spaces, empowering a complete overflow mindset. Demands can consolidate prosperity, associations, and in everyday flourishing. By perceiving flood in various pieces of life, individuals foster a mindset that attracts accomplishment on various fronts.

Following Progression: Affirmation Journals and Reflections

Keeping an affirmation journal gives an undeniable record of the overflow adventure. Customary reflections on progress, standpoint moves, and propelling targets develop the practicality of affirmations. It's connected to making a recorded story of the phenomenal power of positive thinking on money related results.

Creating Appreciation Nearby Certificates: A Synergistic System

Appreciation and demands structure an agreeable relationship. Integrating appreciation practices into verification customs overhauls their ampleness. Offering gratitude for current money related favors makes a positive vibration that lines up with the certificates for future wealth.

Affirmation Practices in Friendly scenes: Total Energy

Partaking in bundle attestation practices handles total energy. Whether in studios, online organizations, or with close circles, shared affirmations make a helpful energy that upgrades their impact. The total point intensifies the vibrational repeat of positive confirmations.

Changing Certificates to Creating Goals: A Remarkable Cycle

As money related goals grow, so should certificates. Reliably examining and changing demands ensures they line up with current cravings. This strong course of refinement keeps the statement customs significant and solid in driving constant overflow creation.

Reasonable Snares and Courses of action: Investigating Challenges

While solid, validation customs can encounter ensnarements. Typical hardships consolidate anomaly, nonappearance of significant affiliation, and assurance from validations. Plans incorporate refining demands for up close and personal resonation, tending to limiting convictions through additional practices, and brainstorming philosophies for consistent blend into everyday presence.

Legitimate Perspectives on Demands: The Mind Body Affiliation

Legitimate assessments endorse the mind body relationship in affirmation practices. Research recommends that positive demands can affect mind associations, decline strain, and add to for the most part flourishing. Understanding the science behind demands adds a layer of precise assistance to their exceptional potential.

Everyday Demands as the Organizer of Overflow Viewpoint

In the ensemble of overflow creation, ordinary affirmation customs emerge as the organizer of the overflow mindset. These functions, when moved closer with objective, consistency, and up close and personal resonation, become the foundation whereupon financial flood is built. They transcend basic words, transforming into a strong power that reshapes contemplations, convictions, and exercises.

The journey of making a viewpoint of flood through regular demands is a singular odyssey, unique to each individual's targets and desires. As you leave on this pivotal practice, may your affirmations resonate with the repeat of wealth, making an appealing move that effectively attracts financial thriving into your life. Everyday certificate customs for overflow are not just a preparation; they are a pathway to changing the mind into an endless money magnet, coordinating an outfit of flood that resonations through each piece of your financial journey.

CHAPTER 5:

Procedures for Drawing in Valuable open doors

In the extraordinary weaving of individual and master development, the ability to attract important entryways stays as an establishment for progress. It goes past chance encounters; it incorporates a cognizant and imperative method for managing adjusting to conditions that incite improvement and prospering. We ought to dive straight into the middle frameworks for attracting open entryways, loosening up the strings that network achievement into the surface of one's outing.

1. Clarity of Vision: Portray Your North Star

Significant entryways are drawn to those with an indisputable internal compass and heading. Begin by portraying your vision — what do you attempt to achieve? Clearness transforms into the coordinating light that attracts open entryways agreed with your targets. Whether in your calling, business, or individual life, a described North Star goes probably as an alluring power, pulling in significant entryways that resound with your vision.

2. Constant Learning: The Cash of Adaptability

The world is in endless development, and astounding entryways every now and again ride the surges of progress. Embrace steady progressing as the cash of adaptability. Stay curious, put assets into your capacities, and be responsive to industry designs. A mindset of predictable improvement positions you as a magnet for expected open entryways, as you are ready to investigate creating scenes easily.

3. Coordinating Strength: Produce Confirmed Affiliations

Getting sorted out is more than exchanging business cards; it's connected to designing credible affiliations. Open entryways much of the time arise through associations in view of trust and normal benefit. Go to industry events, participate in electronic organizations, and backing capable associations. A strong association transforms into a productive ground where potential entryways develop and flourish.

4. Proactive Decisive reasoning: Expect and Address Troubles

Open entryways much of the time hide away inside challenges. Foster a proactive decisive reasoning mindset. Anticipate likely impediments in your industry or field, and position yourself as the plan. Whether it's streamlining processes, introducing improvements, or having a tendency to pain points, the ability to deal with issues positions you as a go-to resource for potential entryways searching for objective.

5. Crucial Bet Taking: Decided Conviction based moves

141

Significant entryways are just now and again tracked down in safe spots. Embrace key bet taking as a method for opening new doorways. This doesn't recommend wild decisions; rather, it incorporates decided conviction based moves. Assess possibilities, weigh potential rewards, and step into the dark whenever the potential for opportunity calls.

6. Checking Significance: Position Yourself as a Subject matter expert

Open entryways float towards those evident as experts in their field. Build an individual or master brand that reflects significance. Show off your expertise through thought drive, quality work, and a consistent brand presence. A strong brand attracts important entryways as well as positions you as the most ideal choice when they arise.

7. The ability to see the value in anybody at their center: Investigate Associations Effectively

Open entryways much of the time emerge inside the area of human correspondences. Encourage ability to see the value in anybody at their center to investigate associations effectively. Sort out the necessities, motivations, and stresses of others. Effective correspondence and sympathy set out an environment where open entryways regularly surface, driven by bona fide affiliations and understanding.

8. Flexibility and Adaptability: Turn with Ease

In an extraordinary world, the ability to turn with magnificence opens approaches to unexpected entryways. Be versatile in your approach, prepared to acclimate to developing circumstances. Inflexible nature can confine your ability to rapidly make the most of chances that emerge outside your basic game plan.

Embrace change as an impulse for new and surprising possible results.

9. Adaptability in Setbacks: Open entryways Disguised as Challenges

Disasters are not street obstacles yet rather reroutes inciting startling entryways. Foster adaptability even with troubles. The ability to get back from adversities positions you to uncover potential entryways that may be hidden as hindrances. Acquire from dissatisfactions, shift your direction, and view hardships as wandering stones to advance.

10. Thought Drive: Crane Your Industry Presence

Potential entryways regularly pound on the doorways of thought pioneers. Lift your industry presence by transforming into a voice of force. Share pieces of information, add to discussions, and successfully participate in trim the tale of your field. Thought managerial jobs you as a magnet for open entryways, as your expertise transforms into an aide in your industry.

11. Agreeable Attitude: Search for Common advantage Affiliations

Joint exertion broadens the horizons of possibility. Take on a helpful standpoint, searching for common advantage associations. Potential entryways routinely arise through joint undertakings, facilitated endeavors, and affiliations where the united characteristics of individuals or affiliations make a helpful energy that attracts progress.

12. Resonation with Values: Change Astounding opportunities to Core value

Not all entryways are made same. Channel open entryways according to the viewpoint of your fundamental convictions. Changing your inclinations to values ensures that the entryways you attract resonate with your authentic self. This course of action overhauls fulfillment as well as attracts open entryways that contribute vehemently to your own and capable journey.

13. Proactive Frameworks organization: Plant Seeds for Future Entryways

Getting sorted out is positively not an inert endeavor; it incorporates proactive responsibility. Plant seeds for future entryways by dependably supporting associations. Return again to contacts, express genuine interest in their endeavors, and be accessible in the master natural framework. Proactive frameworks organization makes a ready ground where potential entryways regularly sprout long term.

14. Discernment and Appearance: Attract Potential entryways Deliberately

The power of discernment and appearance can't be underestimated. Envision the potential entryways you search for. Make a mental image of your optimal outcomes, and let this discernment guide your exercises. By deliberately attracting open entryways through focused thought, you become a co-producer of the circumstances that lead to advance.

15. Appreciation Practices: Accuse Significant entryways of Thankfulness

Practicing appreciation fills in as a magnet for significant entryways. Offer gratitude for existing gifts, constant entryways, and the ones on the way. A mindset of appreciation makes a positive vibrational repeat that attracts extra inspirations to be grateful — potential entryways included.

The Workmanship and Investigation of Chance Interest

In the novel dance of life, the craftsmanship and investigation of attracting potential entryways become a phenomenal power. It's about more than karma or karma; it incorporates a cognizant and indispensable method for managing arranging oneself for progress. As you do these methods, remember that potential entryways are

147

not erratic occasions — they are the ordinary consequence of a conscious and reason driven mindset. May your cycle be stacked up with doorways opening, ways spreading out, and a consistent movement of chances that line up with your vision of progress.

Perceiving and Taking advantage of Monetary Chances

In the continuously creating scene of cash, the ability to see and make the most of chances is the foundation to making and broadening monetary steadiness. Significant entryways don't really for each situation proclaim themselves; often, they present as unpretentious signs or dismissed ways. To investigate this money related scene really, one ought to encourage a sharp eye for seeing these expected entryways and the deftness to clutch them when they arise.

Getting a handle on Money related Open entryways: The Supporting of Overflow Creation

At its middle, seeing money related open entryways incorporates understanding the components of the market, industry designs, and the greater monetary scene. It's connected to staying educated, coordinating cautious investigation, and being delicate to the factors that drive money related advancements. This major data transforms into the point of convergence through which potential entryways come into focus.

Market Assessment: Unraveling Examples and Models

A critical piece of seeing financial entryways lies in market assessment. This incorporates interpreting examples and models inside the monetary trade, land, or any endeavor vehicle. Whether through particular assessment, head examination, or a mix of both, understanding business area components engages individuals to recognize conceivable entryways for improvement or adventure.

Monetary Markers: Investigating the Financial Scene

Financial markers go about as guideposts in seeing money related open entryways. Noticing pointers, for instance, GDP advancement, joblessness rates, and extension gives encounters into the by and large prosperity. Changes in these markers can hail potential hypothesis significant entryways or locales for money related change.

Risk Assessment: Changing Danger and Grant

Seeing money related open entryways requires a sharp sensation of danger assessment. While astounding entryways habitually go with the potential for compensation, they in like manner convey natural risks. Surveying the bet to-repay extent is principal in choosing if an entryway lines up with one's money related targets and risk obstruction.

Mechanical Degrees of progress: Embracing Headway

In the contemporary financial scene, mechanical movements frequently achieve new entryways. Whether it's placing assets into emerging progressions, examining fintech plans, or using the benefits of man-made thinking, seeing important entryways inside the space of improvement is an indication of money related sharpness.

Ambitious Undertakings: Perceiving Business Important entryways

For those with a spearheading soul, seeing money related open entryways much of the time incorporates separating openings watching out or disregarded needs. Productive business visionaries particularly notice buyer lead, market demands, and emerging examples to pinpoint open entryways for shipping off or expanding associations.

Land Significant entryways: Taking advantage of Property Markets

151

The real estate market offers a productive ground for money related open entryways. Seeing anticipated in misjudged properties, emerging areas, or locales going through progress can provoke useful land hypotheses. Timing and understanding area monetary circumstances are basic in making the most of land possibilities.

Financial Preparation: Drawing in Open entryway Affirmation

Placing assets into financial preparation is an interest in the ability to see open entryways. Sorting out money related instruments, adventure procedures, and laying out long haul monetary strength principles outfits individuals with the data expected to perceive and profit from open entryways in various financial regions.

Frameworks organization and Information Stream: Using Affiliations

In the interconnected universe of cash, coordinating expects a urgent part in seeing financial entryways. Attracting with specialists, going to industry events, and partaking in financial organizations make streets for information stream. Pieces of information shared inside associations can every now and again go about as early indications of likely entryways.

Flexibility in Adventure Frameworks: Acclimating to Market Changes

Financial business areas are dynamic, and seeing entryways requires adaptability in hypothesis strategies. Being willing to change portfolios, examine new pursuit vehicles, or widen assets considering changing financial circumstances is basic to rapidly making the most of creating money related possibilities.

Overall Perspectives: Developing Horizons

An overall perspective grows the degree of money related open entryways. Seeing the capacity of overall business areas, getting a handle on overall money related examples, and examining cross-line hypotheses can open approaches to various and conceivably remunerating financial entryways.

Financial Planning: Changing Entryways to Targets

Convincing financial organizing fills in as an aide for seeing and making the most of possibilities. Clearly described financial goals give a framework to surveying open entryways to the extent that how well they line up with one's general targets. This fundamental philosophy ensures that important entryways add to the greater money related course of action.

Lead Monetary issues: Sorting out Mental Factors

Seeing money related open entryways isn't solely about numbers and examples; it furthermore incorporates grasping the psychological factors that influence route. Social monetary viewpoints researches what mental inclinations and sentiments mean for money related choices. Seeing and easing these tendencies works on one's ability to reach informed decisions about money related open entryways.

Government Methodologies and Rules: Investigating Legitimate Frameworks

Government methodologies and rules expect a basic part in trim financial scenes. Observing changes in control guidelines, financial lift packs, or authoritative developments can uncover open entryways. Of course, understanding potential perils related with system changes is fundamental in making informed financial decisions.

Timing and Resilience: Holding on for the Right Second

Timing is by and large an essential figure seeing and making the most of financial possibilities. It incorporates diligence and the ability to keep it together for the right second. Whether it's entering the protections trade during a dive, purchasing land when expenses are positive, or placing assets into a business at its improvement stage, timing can basically impact the result of financial endeavors.

Frameworks organization and Composed exertion: Agreeable Entryways

In the financial area, open entryways every now and again emerge through helpful undertakings. Sorting out with specialists in relating fields, outlining theory get-togethers, or partaking in joint undertakings can open entryways that may not be accessible through free pursuits. Agreeable undertakings impact total data and resources for normal benefit.

Variety to Monetary Cycles: Seeing Examples

Monetary cycles present a scope of possibilities, from regard cash the executives during ruts to taking advantage of improvement periods. Seeing and acclimating to monetary examples positions individuals to investigate the various times of money related cycles, using astonishing entryways exceptional to each stage.

Overall Events and Crises: Changing Hardships into Open entryways

Overall events and crises, while much of the time risky, can similarly set out open entryways. Seeing probably changes in buyer direct, market demands, or emerging endeavors during times of upheaval grants sharp monetary patrons to arrange themselves to make the most of chances that rise out of troubles.

Money related Wellbeing: Preparing for Important entryways

157

Staying aware of money related wellbeing is fundamental to seeing and rapidly making the most of possibilities. Having areas of strength for a foundation, including emergency holds, commitment the chiefs, and an expanded portfolio, gives the robustness expected to acquire by potential entryways when they arise.

A Well established Trip of Financial Entryway Affirmation

In the versatile dance of cash, seeing and rapidly making the most of chances is unquestionably not a specific event anyway a dependable trip. It requires a blend of data, intuition, flexibility, and key thinking. Whether in the protections trade, land, undertaking, or overall hypotheses, the ability to distinguish astonishing entryways and take an unequivocal action clears a path for upheld overflow creation. As you investigate the baffling domain of money related open entryways, may your cycle be separate by a sharp eye, painstakingly thought out game plans, and the fulfillment of your financial longings.

Building Organizations for Monetary Development

In the baffling woven work of art of financial accomplishment, the occupation of associations could never be more critical. Building and supporting huge affiliations is a fundamental starting point for individuals searching for money related improvement. This trip incorporates storing contacts as well as fostering an alternate and strong association that fills in as an impulse for expected open entryways, pieces of information, and helpful undertakings.

Getting a handle on the Power of Associations: Past Restrictive Affiliations

At its substance, getting sorted out is more than a movement of contingent relationship; about building associations make an impetus for all social events included. Seeing the power of associations incorporates understanding that each affiliation is an opportunity for normal turn of events. It's a strong exchange where individuals contribute, group up, and share resources for lift the total financial scene.

The Association Effect: Copying Astounding entryways

The association influence, a thought every now and again associated with advancement, applies every time to money related improvement. As your association expands, the potential for astounding entryways copies emphatically. An overwhelming association doesn't just add direct worth; it has an escalating effect where each new affiliation works on the overall strength and virtuoso of the association.

Fundamental Frameworks organization versus Sum: Quality Matters

Pursuing financial turn of events, the emphasis should be on essential frameworks organization rather than sheer sum. A more unassuming, first class association of strong and trustworthy affiliations can yield more basic results than a tremendous yet shallow overview of contacts. About creating relationship with individuals bring various perspectives, expertise, and entryways to the table.

Assortment in Associations: A Catalyst for Improvement

An alternate association is a wellspring of improvement and improvement. Building relationship with individuals from different endeavors, establishments, and ability districts presents groundbreaking insights and perspectives. Assortment in networks fills in as an impulse for creative decisive reasoning, cross-industry composed endeavors, and the disclosure of capricious financial entryways.

On the web and Detached Frameworks organization: Blending the Most astute situation possible

The old age has expanded frameworks organization open entryways past geological cutoff points. While online frameworks organization stages offer overall reach, standard separated frameworks organization stays critical for empowering further, more extraordinary associations. The best association building strategies every now and again incorporate a genial blend of both on the web and separated coordinated efforts.

Building a Singular Brand: Your Association's First impression

In the area of frameworks organization, your own picture is the first impression you make. Whether through capable achievements, thought drive, or online presence, your own picture shapes how you are seen inside your association. Building a persuading and substantial individual brand positions you as a significant and real person from your money related neighborhood.

Realness in Frameworks organization: Empowering Authentic Affiliations

Realness is the bedrock of critical affiliations. Pursuing money related improvement, realness incorporates being genuine, clear, and predictable with oneself in collaborations. Real getting sorted out develops trust, which is an establishment for persevering through associations and the helpful endeavors that much of the time lead to money related open entryways.

Strategies for Strong Frameworks organization: From Icebreakers to Facilitated exertion

Fruitful frameworks organization is a skill that can be honed through fundamental strategies. From becoming astonishing at colleagues and icebreakers with making persevering through relationship through full focus and resulting meet-ups, there are various procedures for fostering a convincing and critical association.

Moreover, reassuring a helpful standpoint that searches for shared benefit results adds to the life expectancy of association associations.

Mentorship and Frameworks organization: Investigating the Method for advancing

Mentorship is areas of strength for an of frameworks organization that transcends capable heading. A coach offers encounters and insight as well as gives induction to their association, broadening your extension and anticipated open entryways. Spreading out guide mentee associations is a fundamental push toward investigating the way to money related accomplishment.

Coordinating Events and Social affairs: Stages for Affiliation

Participating in frameworks organization events and get-togethers gives dedicated stages to affiliation. Whether industry-express friendly events, profession exhibitions, or master get-togethers, these events offer opportunities to meet comparable individuals, gain from industry trailblazers, and style affiliations that can provoke money related improvement.

Using Virtual Amusement for Frameworks organization: Past LinkedIn

Virtual diversion stages, past the inescapable LinkedIn, offer huge entryways for frameworks organization. Taking part in industry-related conversations on Twitter, displaying fitness on Instagram, or participating in capable social events on Facebook can overhaul your electronic presence and attract affiliations that line up with your financial targets.

Putting together Propriety: Investigating Capable Joint efforts

Putting together propriety is a basic piece of building getting through affiliations. From ideal and appreciative correspondence to with respect to others' time and cutoff points, seeing genuine habits works on your remaining inside your association. Thoughtful gestures, for instance, offering thanks or offering assistance, add to the positive components of your money related affiliations.

Network Upkeep: Consistency is Basic

Building an association is a persistent cycle that requires consistent effort. Reliably checking in with affiliations, giving updates on your master cycle, and offering support when expected add to the upkeep of a prospering association. Consistency develops trust and develops the equivalent thought of critical affiliations.

Changing Relationship into Facilitated endeavors: The Helpful Advantage

The real power of an association lies in the affiliations you put forth as well as in the organized attempts that come from those affiliations. Changing organization associations into helpful undertakings upgrades the potential for money related advancement. Facilitated endeavors can go from joint undertakings and hypotheses to shared encounters that add to shared achievement.

Coordinating for Spearheading Accomplishment: From Funding to Affiliations

For money managers, getting sorted out is commonly imperative to getting funding, outlining associations, and procuring market encounters. Building relationship with monetary sponsor, industry trained professionals, and potential colleagues can be the way to ambitious accomplishment. Strong frameworks organization in venturesome endeavors incorporates a blend of pitching your vision, showing your dominance, and developing relationship with individuals who can add to your undertaking's turn of events.

Sorting out Troubles and Courses of action: Beating Obstacles

Sorting out, while simultaneously satisfying, goes with its hardships. From overcoming social strain to investigating amassed events, individuals could stand up to hindrances in building affiliations. Plans remember taking for an improvement mindset, searching for help from mentors, and ceaselessly broadening safe spots. Overcoming arranging hardships is an uncommon trip that adds to individual and master development.

Assessing Frameworks organization Accomplishment: Past Quantitative Estimations

Assessing the advancement of frameworks organization tries goes past quantitative estimations. While the size of your association and the amount of affiliations matter, emotional markers like the significance of associations, the level of trust, and the agreeable undertakings that start from your association are comparably critical. Productive frameworks organization is separate by the impact and worth the effort brings to your financial outing.

Organizing for Professional success: Ascending the Company pecking order

In a corporate setting, organizing is an amazing asset for professional success. Building associations inside and outside the association upgrades perceivability, opens ways to new open doors, and positions people for advancements or key profession moves. Organizing for professional success includes interfacing with bosses as well as developing associations with companions, coaches, and industry powerhouses.

Coordinating in the Gig Economy: Making a Virtual Gathering

As the gig economy continues to prosper, arranging takes on another perspective. Trained professionals and independent specialists can make virtual gatherings through frameworks organization, collaborating on projects, and suggesting each other for open entryways. Building an association of advisors with relating capacities develops the extent of organizations one can offer and works on financial potential outcomes in the gig economy.

Overall Frameworks organization: Past Limits for Worldwide Entryways

In an interconnected world, overall frameworks organization opens approaches to worldwide entryways. Attracting with specialists from different countries, partaking in overall conversations, and using on the web stages work with cross-line affiliations. Overall frameworks organization extends perspectives along with opens different financial entryways in a globalized economy.

Coordinating and The ability to see the value in anybody at their center: Building Social Capital

The ability to comprehend people on a more profound level is a groundwork of strong frameworks organization. Being open to others' sentiments, practicing compassion, and investigating social components with responsiveness add to building social capital.

The capacity to see the value in individuals on a more profound level works on the idea of affiliations and develops an environment where critical facilitated endeavors can succeed.

Overcoming Frameworks organization Burnout: Changing Sum and Quality

While frameworks organization is instrumental for financial turn of events, beyond preposterous frameworks organization can provoke burnout. Changing the sum and nature of affiliations is basic to doing whatever it takes not to organize weariness. Focusing in on associations that line up with your targets, zeroing in on critical collaborations, and setting sensible suppositions add to a legitimate and fruitful frameworks organization approach.

The Always Growing Embroidery of Monetary Associations

Building networks is a craftsmanship that creates with each new association in the consistently extending embroidery of monetary development. It's a strong outing of creating associations,

171

empowering joint endeavors, and investigating the interconnected snare of possibilities. As you weave your association, may it be a dynamic and reliably creating weaving that adds to your money related achievement as well as overhauls the total flourishing of those inside your financial neighborhood.

CHAPTER 6:

Defeating Cash Blocks

Bringing in cash is frequently attached to our capacity to accommodate ourselves, our families, and our future objectives. Be that as it may, certain individuals experience dread and tension with regards to bringing in cash. This dread might keep them from chasing after rewarding open doors or facing challenges that could yield monetary achievement. On the off chance that you have an anxiety toward bringing in Cash, the following are seven hints to assist you with conquering your cash blocks.

1. Distinguish the base of your trepidation

To conquer your apprehension about bringing in cash, it's fundamental to recognize where it's coming from. You might have a feeling of dread toward progress, disappointment, judgment, committing errors, or something different.

Knowing the foundation of your apprehension can assist you with tending to it more successfully. Invest energy pondering your considerations and sentiments about cash. Are there a particular circumstances or encounters that trigger your trepidation?

2. Challenge your restricting convictions

Many individuals have restricting convictions encompassing cash, for example, "cash is underhanded" or "rich individuals are ravenous." These convictions can keep us away from seeking after monetary development and steadiness. Challenge these convictions by considering elective perspectives and perceiving that cash can be utilized for positive things. Survey your ongoing convictions about cash and work on rethinking them to make an inspirational perspective.

3. Instruct yourself on cash

Having a superior comprehension of funds can assist you with feeling more sure and less unfortunate about bringing in cash. Understand books, take courses, and converse with monetary specialists to acquire information and assemble your abilities. The more you find out about bringing in cash, the more agreeable you will feel accepting dangers and seeking after open doors

4. Make little strides

Begin with little and sensible ways of bringing in cash, for example, taking on a temporary work, selling things you never again need, or accomplishing independent work. As you become more agreeable, you can slowly pursue on greater open doors. Separating your monetary objectives into more modest, feasible errands can assist you with defeating the apprehension about the unexplored world.

5. Encircle yourself with steady individuals

Interface with individuals who have an uplifting outlook towards cash and can offer consolation and direction. Avoid negative or unsupportive people who might build up your apprehension. Organizing with similar people can assist you with building your certainty and furnish you with valuable open doors for development.

6. Envision achievement

Positive perception can assist you with beating your apprehension about bringing in cash. Envision yourself accomplishing your monetary objectives and achieving monetary security. Imagine yourself feeling quiet, sure, and engaged. This can assist you with building a positive mentality towards cash and conquer your trepidation.

7. Practice self-empathy

It's essential to be thoughtful and patient with yourself as you work through your apprehension about bringing in cash. Recollect that it's alright

177

to commit errors and that mishaps are valuable chances to learn and develop. Practice self-sympathy by talking benevolent to yourself, recognizing your advancement, and praising your accomplishments.

Defeating the feeling of dread toward bringing in cash requires a blend of self-reflection, schooling, and activity. By recognizing the foundation of your trepidation, testing your restricting convictions, teaching yourself on cash, making little strides, encircling yourself with strong individuals, picturing achievement, and rehearsing self-empathy, you can start to defeat your cash hinders and make monetary progress in your life.

Keep in mind, bringing in cash is definitely not something frightening. As you work on your feeling of dread toward bringing in cash, you'll face more challenges, and thusly, you'll make more progress. Head with certainty in the path of your monetary dreams and objectives.

Distinguishing and Breaking Cash Restricting Convictions

Your outlook towards cash is a fantastic deciding component with regards to your monetary achievement.

Convictions become considerations, which become activities and these activities frequently support our restricting convictions. For instance, on the off chance that you have a conviction that you are not sufficiently brilliant to be monetarily fruitful you could execute your arrangements with zeal, hit a barrier, question your capacities and surrender. Assuming you accept that it's self centered to need bunches of cash you might undercharge your administrations or offer them for nothing.

The following are 7 exceptionally normal restricting convictions:

- Cash is the foundation of all malevolent

- Needing large chunk of change is narrow minded

- I'm simply bad with cash

- You need to endeavor to get rich
- My family has never been rich

- Cash is there to be spent

- It's more essential to be sound than rich

Do any of these restricting cash convictions impact you? Is it true or not that they are keeping you away from encountering the existence you want?

At the point when I work with my clients we recognize restricting convictions and challenge them. Might it be said that they are valid? If indeed, how might you demonstrate it? Frequently they can't be demonstrated as being valid, or at times bogus... .they are simply convictions.

The subsequent stage we take is to plan methodologies and carry out a monetary activity plan that envelops abundance making exercises and ways of behaving.

These include:

- Setting up a spending plan organizer and understanding how to spending plan - in this manner figuring out HOW to be great with cash

- Figuring out how to deal with your funds so there is sufficient to cover everyday costs, pay down obligation, make investment funds and have some to spend irreproachable - this guarantees that cash is being spent Admirably

- Finding various ways of reducing expenses to divert to abundance speculation - giving a chance to Make

181

your own wealth no matter what your family's ancestry.

- An engaging outcome of being the expert of your cash is that you before long understand not be guaranteed to difficult work makes you rich, yet all things considered, the manner in which you financial plan and deal with your cash.

The blend of attitude and activity is basic for change in all aspects of our lives, and this is particularly apparent with regards to our monetary reality. Pursuing the choice you will reset those restricting convictions that are keeping you down and afterward making a move to deal with your cash will make astounding outcomes. Definitely you can be rich AND cheerful!

Your convictions about cash are framed from numerous things. What you've seen from people around you, similar to relatives and companions, can influence what you think today.

You may likewise have gathered convictions or considerations about cash from your own encounters with it. Be that as it may, those convictions aren't generally the best ones.

In some cases they are poisonous or restricting convictions about cash, as a matter of fact. How might you let know if you accept whatever is keeping you down?

Furthermore, assuming you do, how would you beat these considerations? Peruse on for thoughts.

What Are Negative Convictions About Cash?

The following are 19 normal convictions about cash that are very negative. Check whether you have at any point trusted any of them yourself. Assuming this is the case, realize that change is conceivable.

1. There isn't sufficient cash to go around.

This may be an idea that whirls to you occasionally. It is exceptionally restricting on the grounds that it reasons that there isn't sufficient cash in that frame of mind for everybody.

That cash is limited, and you can't have a lot of it. This conviction can prevent you from figuring you can procure more.

It might likewise make you feel that something will keep you from accomplishing more.

2. I don't merit huge amount of cash.

This negative conviction fixates on you believing that you're not adequate for cash or, for reasons unknown, don't merit it. This isn't correct!

You might have been directed to this considered on the grounds that past terrible cash propensities, yet that doesn't mean you can't learn and be similarly as equipped for dealing with cash well as any other individual.

3. It is egotistical to Have cash.

Now and again individuals think the rich are underhanded. In fact, there are pleasant rich individuals and mean ones, very much like with all the other things.

It isn't childish to Have cash. You can in any case be liberal and help other people assuming you have cash, perhaps more so than now.

So cash all alone sits idle. It's what you choose to do that matters.

4. It is covetous to Need more cash.

This restricting conviction reasons you shouldn't have any desire to have more cash since it implies you are avaricious. Yet, assuming there is, as a matter of fact, enough cash to go around, and you having more doesn't prevent another person from having cash, it isn't ravenous.

It is great to need to find true success and gain riches. Cash can assist you with doing a ton of incredible things.

5. You really want cash to bring in cash.

While this could validate on certain events, it isn't valid for every one of them. Furthermore, to create financial momentum however have no cash, this conviction can prevent you from getting everything rolling.

The truth of the matter is, you can begin with almost no cash regardless become fruitful utilizing inventiveness and difficult work.

6. You need to hold your cash close.

No matter what the sum you have, holding your cash close can transform into covetousness and monetary uneasiness. In the event that you had very little cash growing up, you may be hesitant to leave behind it.

If all things being equal, you accept that you will have enough and that you can acquire cash from now on, you can decide to face savvy challenges and help individuals with the assets you have now.

7. Having more cash implies I'll have more issues.

Quite possibly of the most restricting conviction about cash is that it makes issues. Cash doesn't make issues; that is simply aspect of life.

ave riches, as cash can likewise settle a few issues.

8. Cash can't purchase satisfaction.

This is consistent with a degree. Cash all alone can't purchase joy, yet it can give you significantly more decisions and amazing chances to would things you like to do.

Along these lines, it ought not be stayed away from yet rather ought to be seen for what it is. Not a satisfaction estimation, but rather an instrument that can get you to where you need to be.

9. Cash is difficult to get.
Assuming you think cash is trying to get, you may in all likelihood never attempt in any case. This might keep you in your current situation.

While bringing in cash might take a few work and time, it is absolutely conceivable and doesn't need to be difficult to get.

10. You can't change your monetary future.

This is a finished untruth. As a matter of fact, you are the one in particular who can change your monetary future!

You are completely accountable for how much cash you make, what profession you pick, and how you instruct yourself about cash. You can change your monetary future - no matter what.

11. Cash is the base of wickedness.

This articulation is mistaken, and really, it peruses, "For the love of cash is a base of a wide range of insidiousness." Intending that permitting cash to turn into your most esteemed belonging can adversely transform you.

In any case, that doesn't imply that cash is terrible. You can likewise have cash and be a liberal and kind individual. Simply don't bring in cash the focal point of for what seems like forever.

12. I'm bad with cash.

Nobody is conceived great with cash. We figure out how to deal with it well or inadequately from others and from what we know all alone.

That implies you can teach and prepare yourself to deal with cash decidedly, similarly as effectively as in a negative way.

While some might be naturally introduced to great monetary circumstances, and others aren't, you can in any case assume command over your future and realize all you can about back. You can then figure out how to be bad, yet incredible, with cash.

13. Overseeing cash is an excess of stress.

This is one of the restricting convictions about cash that is altogether in reverse. In reality, not overseeing cash is unpleasant.
Cash is essential for our lives regardless. So overlooking it or dealing with it ineffectively can cause tension. Then again, having an arrangement and sorting out your funds might cause less pressure.

14. Cash was intended for spending.

Cash is intended for bunches of things. Spending is one of them, yet assuming that is all you do with it, you will pass up having a sound monetary future.

Cash is additionally implied for saving, effective financial planning, and giving. There are what should be done with it, and being shrewd about how you handle it is really smart.

15. I can't set aside cash.

Regardless of whether you have never saved a penny in all your years, indeed, you can set aside cash! It involves discipline and an arrangement, yet all at once it's conceivable.

Setting aside cash gives you a lot more choices and assists you with being secure with finance later on. So figure out how to set aside cash to carry on with life in the most effective way conceivable.

16. In the event that I have an excessive amount of cash, I'll lose my qualities.

Cash doesn't give values. This returns to the negative conviction that cash is malevolent.
Cash does nothing all alone, as a matter of fact. We give it esteem and pick the way things are spent and saved.
So no, being rich won't cause you to lose your qualities. You have total control over that.

17. I can't cherish my vocation and rake in boatloads of cash.

Assuming you love what you do, it should not make you any cash, correct? Wrong!
You can find a profession you appreciate, have an effect, and bring in cash all the while. There are about a zillion ways of bringing in cash, and you can in any case make abundance in any event, when you like your work.

18. I won't ever have sufficient cash.

Certain individuals view cash as security, yet believing that you won't ever have enough isn't accurate.

You want cash to live and be ready for the future and crises. Past that, perceive that you do have enough.

19. My family has forever been poor.

Since history says one thing doesn't imply that is what's to come. Past doesn't direct present or future.

All things being equal, decide to accept that regardless of how much or minimal expenditure your family has, you can choose your own monetary fate. Then, it requires investing the energy and sorting out the moves toward take a different path.

Clearing Mental Hindrances to Overflow

Find the groundbreaking influence of the abundance attitude! Beat mental hindrances to success with reasonable techniques. Release your maximum capacity and make monetary progress today.

In the immense scene of human accomplishment, scarcely any undertakings spellbind the creative mind very like the journey for success.

We as a whole long for a daily existence loaded up with overflow, satisfaction, and monetary security. However, as a general rule, our excursion towards thriving is obstructed by undetectable hindrances — boundaries that exist not in the outside world, but rather inside our own personalities. This is where the abundance outlook enters the stage as a strong power of change. In this release, we figure out the abundance outlook, take apart the psychological hindrances that block our way to flourishing, and reveal useful techniques for developing a mentality of overflow in view of genuine encounters.

The idea of abundance frequently invokes pictures of spilling over financial balances, rich homes, and extravagant vehicles.

A depiction has been imbued in our psyches for ages. However, imagine a scenario in which I enlightened you that abundance isn't exclusively concerning cash, yet a perspective — an outlook that can open endless open doors and thriving.

Grasping the Abundance Outlook

Envision remaining on the edge of a lavish, rambling plantation, with organic product loaded trees extending as may be obvious.

This plantation addresses overflow — the foundation of the abundance attitude. The people who embrace this attitude trust that open doors, assets, and abundance resemble the organic product in the plantation — boundless.

They don't capitulate to the shortage attitude that shackles so many.

Each tree in this plantation bears the product of chance. This plantation represents the embodiment of the abundance mentality — an enduring faith in overflow.

It's the grasping that open doors, assets, and abundance are not limited products, but rather an always streaming waterway of bounty.

Overflow Thinking:
The abundance mentality flourishes with overflow thinking, which is the conviction that there is all that could possibly be needed to go around. It is the absolute opposite of shortage thinking, which breeds dread, wavering, and botched open doors.

The people who embrace this attitude trust that open doors, assets, and abundance resemble the organic product in the plantation — boundless.

They don't capitulate to the shortage attitude that shackles so many.

Monetary Proficiency:

Grasping cash, ventures, and monetary arranging is key to the abundance outlook. It includes ceaseless learning and informed direction in regards to your funds.

Positive Self-esteem:

People with an abundance outlook have a sound self-esteem that isn't tied exclusively to their monetary achievement. They perceive their worth past money related accomplishments.

Objective Situated:

Putting forth and chasing after clear monetary objectives is a sign of the abundance outlook. These objectives are tied in with gathering abundance as well as about accomplishing monetary security and making a significant life.

Mental Hindrances to Success

Presently, we should travel through the plantation of the psyche and uncover the stones that discourage the way to thriving. To conquer mental hindrances, we should initially recognize and grasp them.

The Viewpoint that everything is limited

Envision being caught in a little, dull room without any windows or entryways.

This is the psychological jail of the world view limited by fear. It is the conviction that assets are restricted, potential open doors are scant, and achievement is a lose situation.

This conviction frequently prompts dread driven independent direction, making us contract from possible open doors.

The Feeling of dread toward Disappointment

Dread frequently remains as the guard to flourishing, keeping us from jumping all over chances and understanding our maximum capacity.

The irritating voice murmurs, "Imagine a scenario in which you fizzle?" and deadens us in our tracks with self-question. However, it's memorable's pivotal that trepidation, in its embodiment, is a courier — a sign that we are getting out of our usual range of familiarity.

The feeling of dread toward disappointment assumes the part of the main bad guy.
This dread keeps us from proceeding with well balanced plans of action, chasing after aggressive objectives, and eventually, from understanding our maximum capacity.

Negative Self-Talk
Envision a mirror that mirrors your actual appearance as well as reverberations your inward contemplations and self-esteem.

Negative self-talk is similar to a broken mirror, contorting our mental self view and hindering our certainty.

199

At the point when we continually criticize ourselves, we sabotage our capacity to jump all over chances and develop success.

Absence of Monetary Education
In our advanced world, monetary education is the compass that guides us through the maze of individual accounting.

However, numerous people find themselves afloat, without the information and abilities expected to pursue informed monetary choices.

This absence of monetary proficiency can prompt unfortunate cash the executives and block our excursion toward flourishing.

Systems for Developing an Abundance Mentality

Since we have distinguished these psychological hindrances, we should explore the plantation of the brain and find the apparatuses that can assist us with making the way to flourishing:

Embrace Overflow Thinking

To battle the viewpoint that everything is limited, we should sincerely embrace overflow thinking.

Begin by rehearsing appreciation for what you have and recognizing the vast conceivable outcomes that look for you. This change in context is the most important move towards developing an abundance outlook.

Face Dread Head-On

Dread isn't our foe; a gatekeeper signals development.

Rather than avoiding dread, face it head-on. Comprehend that dread is a characteristic piece of the excursion towards flourishing.

The fuel drives us to go ahead with reasonable plans of action and embrace new open doors.

Outfit the Force of Positive Self-Talk

Envision your psyche as a rich nursery where each thought sows a seed.
Supplant self-analysis with positive confirmations that support your self-esteem and self-conviction.
The more you attest your capacities, the more you engage yourself to accomplish flourishing.

Positive insistences are the instruments to reshape our self-talk. They supplant self-uncertainty with certainty, developing a prolific ground for thriving to prosper.

Focus on Deep rooted Learning
In the abundance mentality plantation, there's a heavily wooded with information, ready to go. It represents the significance of monetary proficiency.

Figuring out cash, ventures, and monetary arranging isn't an extravagance; it's a need.

Monetary proficiency is the light that enlightens the way to monetary flourishing. Focus on deep rooted finding out about cash the executives, speculations, and monetary preparation.

Understand books, go to classes, and look for counsel from monetary specialists. Information is the key that opens monetary entryways.

Put forth Clear and Intentional Objectives

A boat cruising without an objective is unfastened. Likewise, an existence without clear monetary objectives needs heading.

Put forth clear cut monetary objectives, both present moment and long haul.
Stall down into noteworthy stages and make a guide to direct your excursion to success.

Encircle Yourself with Energy

Imagine the abundance mentality plantation as a social event place for similar people.
Individuals you encircle yourself with can either support or obstruct your outlook. Encircling yourself with energy and consolation can support your convictions and aspirations.

Encircle yourself with people who share the abundance outlook.

Join organizations, gatherings, or associations that energize energy, move development, and support your convictions and aspirations.

The Way of Flourishing

The abundance outlook is definitely not an enchanted spell that in a split second changes your life.

It's an excursion — an intentional and cognizant work to reshape your viewpoint, destroy mental hindrances, and develop enabling convictions

By embracing overflow, facing dread, sustaining positive self-talk, focusing on long lasting picking up, putting forth clear objectives, and encircling yourself with inspiration, you will clear a way towards a prosperous future.

Keep in mind, abundance isn't restricted to the limits of a bank proclamation; it reaches out into the domain of bountiful living, satisfied dreams, and significant reason.

The abundance mentality is the way to open this uncommon universe of thriving — an existence where your potential has no limits.

Thus, venture out into the plantation of overflow, and let your mentality be the compass that guides you on this exhilarating excursion toward abundance in the entirety of its structures. Flourishing anticipates the people who try to embrace it.

CHAPTER 7:

Care in Speculation and Growing a strong financial foundation

Understanding the intricate details of individual accounting is a fundamental ability that impacts our solace, security, and the capacity to satisfy our fantasies and yearnings.

The monetary arranging that we embrace today establishes the groundwork for a protected tomorrow. However, however much it is about numbers and computations, monetary arranging is additionally about making the daily routine that we wish to experience. Thus, beginning from the get-go in this excursion is pivotal as it gives a more extensive time skyline to create financial momentum and pad oneself against life's vulnerabilities.

Notwithstanding, monetary arranging can frequently feel upsetting, which is the reason it is vital to take on an all encompassing and careful way to deal with it; a way that permits us to develop our riches and meet our objectives without settling on inner harmony.

Here is an outline of what to think about while making a comprehensive monetary arrangement.

Decide your monetary objectives:

The first and most significant stage in any monetary arrangement is to recognize your monetary objectives. A monetary objectives organizer isn't simply a record; it is a bunch of techniques custom-made to focus on and accomplish one's ideal monetary results. From momentary goals like arranging a get-away to long haul desires, for example, guaranteeing an agreeable retirement, it is critical to set clear and practical targets. Understanding how to accomplish monetary objectives begins with arranging them into present moment, medium-term, and long haul, each requiring various systems and monetary instruments.

Make a spending plan:

Making a spending plan is the outline for monetary achievement. It's tied in with adjusting your pay against your costs to guarantee you live inside your means while financial planning for what's in store. A powerful financial plan can follow your spending designs, assist you with eliminating unimportant costs, and permit you to efficiently allot assets towards your objectives.

Just-in-case account:

We can set up all we like, however life doesn't generally go as per the arrangement. A rainy day account is your monetary security net, intended to cover surprising costs like health related crises or unexpected employment cutback. In a perfect world, it ought to cover three to a half year of everyday costs, kept in a promptly open structure like a fluid asset.

Making arrangements for retirement:

Retirement might appear to be far off, however making arrangements for it is perhaps of the main monetary objective. Beginning early can have the effect between resigning in solace or confronting monetary difficulties during your brilliant years. Adding to a retirement asset or putting resources into benefits plans guarantees that you have a consistent progression of pay when you never again get a customary check.

Putting resources into what's in store:

The expense of schooling is steadily rising, and beginning to save ahead of schedule for your kid's schooling can ease monetary weight from now on. Use instruments like training investment funds plans or shared reserves that offer great returns over a significant stretch.

Contributing to develop your riches:

While saving is fundamental, contributing truly develops your abundance. Broaden your ventures across resources like stocks, securities, shared assets, and land to streamline the return potential while overseeing gambles. This approach permits your cash to beat expansion successfully over the long haul and develop your abundance throughout the long term.

Anticipating large buys:

Any huge buy, such as purchasing a home, requires critical capital, which can frequently make the requirement for a credit. Monetary making arrangements for such buys includes putting something aside for up front installments, understanding credit terms, and guaranteeing that you have the pay to oversee reimbursements without stressing your funds.

Charge productivity:

Keeping a greater amount of what you procure: One of the vital components of monetary arranging is understanding and utilizing charge saving choices. Charge proficiency is tied in with organizing your interests in a way that limits charge liabilities lawfully. It guarantees that you keep a greater amount of what you procure, and your speculations keep on developing.

Talking with a monetary counsel:

While self-arranging is great, talking with a monetary counsel can offer master experiences customized to your monetary circumstance. Counsels can offer a comprehensive way to deal with monetary preparation, ensuring that all parts of your monetary life are equipped towards accomplishing your objectives.

Embracing a careful way to deal with monetary arranging goes past gathering riches. It includes adjusting your monetary practices to your life values, so every monetary choice backings your general life objectives. It is a persistent course of assessment and correction to keep your funds in line with the progressions in your day to day existence.

Monetary arranging isn't just an undertaking yet an excursion towards monetary freedom and satisfaction. By doing things like defining clear monetary objectives, making a nitty gritty spending plan, getting ready for crises, putting something aside for retirement, and contributing carefully, you can embrace this excursion effectively. It is critical to recall that a comprehensive way to deal with monetary arranging isn't just about arriving at an objective; it is as much about partaking in the excursion, furnished with the true serenity that comes from monetary security.

FAQs:

How could care rehearses further develop my monetary prosperity?
Care can upgrade monetary direction by advancing familiarity with ways of managing money, lessening rash buys, and encouraging a more profound comprehension of the association among values and cash.

Could care at any point assist with long haul monetary preparation and objective setting?

Indeed. Care can help in defining sensible monetary objectives, developing tolerance for long haul results, and encouraging versatility even with monetary difficulties.

Common Asset ventures are likely to advertise gambles, read all plan related archives cautiously.

This archive ought not be treated as an underwriting of the perspectives/suppositions or as venture exhortation. This record ought not be interpreted as an examination report or a suggestion to trade any security. This report is for data purposes just and ought not be understood as a commitment on least returns or shield of capital. This archive alone isn't adequate and ought not be utilized for the turn of events or execution of a speculation technique. The beneficiary ought to note and comprehend that the data gave above may not contain every one of the material viewpoints pertinent for pursuing a speculation choice. Financial backers are encouraged to counsel their own venture consultant prior to settling on any speculation choice considering their gamble craving, venture objectives and skyline. This data is dependent on future developments with no earlier notification.

Shrewd Financial planning with a Careful Methodology

As we have seen with past "Dark Swan" occasions and Coronavirus instigates monetary emergency, what's to come is flighty. Nonetheless, how one answers vulnerability can be arranged ahead of time. Emergency Contributing is a basic part of creating financial momentum and getting a prosperous future. Nonetheless, the universe of money management can be intricate and overpowering, frequently enticing financial backers to pursue imprudent choices driven by momentary additions. To explore the speculation scene effectively, taking on a smart and restrained approach is vital. There are many key rules that a smart financial

214

backer keeps while effective financial planning, intending to boost returns while overseeing gambles really.

Prior to setting out on a venture, characterizing clear monetary goals is fundamental. Whether it's putting something aside for retirement, financing instruction, or purchasing a home, having explicit targets gives guidance and designates assets in like manner. By understanding your speculation objectives, you can tailor your venture methodology to line up with your drawn out goals.

1-Broaden Your Portfolio

The familiar proverb of "don't tie up your assets in one place" turns out as expected in money management. Broadening is a fundamental rule that oversees risk and safeguard your capital. By spreading speculations across various resource classes, areas, and topographical districts, you can moderate the effect of any single venture's underperformance. A very much enhanced portfolio can assist with catching increases from different sources while padding likely misfortunes.

2-Do Exhaustive Exploration

A smart financial backer behaviors thorough examination prior to pursuing any speculation choice. This includes dissecting the monetary strength of organizations, surveying industry patterns, and figuring out macroeconomic variables. Remaining informed about market elements, perusing monetary reports, and following well-qualified feelings empowers financial backers to go with very much educated decisions. Keep in mind, information is power with regards to effective financial planning.

3-Create financial wellbeing over the Long haul with patient and discipline

Effective financial planning is a long distance race, not a run. Smart financial backers have a drawn out viewpoint, understanding that markets can be unstable in the short run. By zeroing in on the basics of their ventures and opposing the impulse to pursue fast gains, they keep away from automatic responses to advertise vacillations. Persistence and discipline are critical to enduring business sector highs and lows and accomplishing maintainable development over the long run.

4-Embrace Chance Administration

Contributing innately implies risk, yet an insightful financial backer knows how to successfully oversee it. This guideline involves grasping one's gamble resistance and thinking up a speculation system that lines up with it. Smart financial backers enhance their portfolios, set proper resource assignment targets, and intermittently rebalance their possessions. Moreover, they utilize procedures, for example, setting stop-misfortune arranges and having a rainy day account to pad against unforeseen monetary mishaps.

-Establishment block

-Saves safe cash worth a year of costs in a fluid asset like Quantum fluid asset.

-Risk lessening block

-Development Block

5-Stay away from Profound Navigation

Feelings can be the ruin of numerous financial backers. A smart financial backer remaining parts normal and tries not to settle on imprudent choices driven by dread or ravenousness. Feeling driven activities frequently lead to purchasing at market pinnacles and selling during slumps, bringing about misfortunes. By keeping a trained methodology and adhering to a thoroughly examined money growth strategy, financial backers can keep feelings from obfuscating their judgment.

6-Look past conventional methodologies of buying Gold

While gold's true capacity for protecting worth over the long haul is known to all, smart financial backers are additionally mindful of its portfolio expanding job that limits disadvantage takes a chance during times of macroeconomic vulnerability.

7-Routinely Survey and Change

The venture scene is dynamic, and remaining careful is vital. A smart financial backer occasionally surveys their portfolio's presentation, reevaluates their objectives, and changes their methodology on a case by case basis. Customary portfolio audits help recognize failing to meet expectations speculations and valuable open doors for rebalancing. By remaining proactive, financial backers can guarantee their ventures stay lined up with their drawn out goals.

Contributing is both a workmanship and a science, requiring an insightful methodology and

219

adherence to key standards. By defining clear objectives, differentiating portfolios, leading exhaustive examination, contributing as long as possible, embracing risk the executives, staying away from close to home independent direction, and routinely investigating and changing procedures, financial backers can explore the intricacies of the market effectively. Keep in mind, smart money management isn't tied in with pursuing for the time being wealth yet rather about making a strong starting point for long haul monetary achievement.

Developing Your Abundance with Tolerance and Reason

In the speedy universe of today, where moment satisfaction is much of the time the standard, the specialty of tolerance in growing long term financial stability is regularly neglected. However, it stays a basic support point for anybody seeking to turn into a tycoon from nothing. Persistence isn't simply pausing; it's a vital, restrained way to deal with making long haul monetary progress.

Understanding the Job of Time in Establishing long term financial stability

The excursion to turning into a tycoon isn't a run; it's a long distance race. One of the basic slip-ups many individuals make is looking for handy solutions and quick gains. While these could offer brief fulfillment, they frequently need maintainability and can prompt hazardous choices. Abundance worked over the long run, then again, will in general be stronger and persevering.

The Benefit of Learning and Developing

Tolerance considers a more profound comprehension of the monetary market and individual budget the executives. This period is critical for getting information, understanding business sector patterns, and creating monetary intuition. Each effective financial backer or business visionary will verify the significance of consistent learning and developing. This cycle requires some investment, and racing through it can leave basic holes in one's monetary schooling.

Key Preparation Over Hurried Choices

Abundance creation includes a lot of arranging and strategising. A patient methodology permits you to set clear, feasible objectives and foster a bit by bit intend to contact them. It implies not being influenced by the most recent patterns or friend pressure however rather pursuing choices in light of exploration, examination, and your drawn out monetary goals.

Genuine Examples of overcoming adversity

Consider the accounts of fruitful people who have created their financial stability over the long haul. They frequently share a typical topic: they didn't accomplish their monetary objectives short-term. All things considered, they worked constantly, went with determined choices, and permitted their speculations to develop. These accounts act as strong updates that tolerance is without a doubt a righteousness in the domain of monetary achievement.

Embracing Persistence in Your Monetary Excursion

To develop persistence, begin by setting sensible assumptions. Comprehend that abundance creation is a steady cycle. Planning, saving, and contributing shrewdly are portions of this interaction. Celebrate little triumphs en route and gain from mishaps without getting deterred.

The Reality

Persistence in growing a strong financial foundation is something other than pausing; it's about smart preparation, ceaseless learning, and permitting your ventures to develop. In a world that frequently focuses on speed over solidness, picking the way of persistence can separate you on your excursion to turning into a mogul. Keep in mind, the most getting through victories are those that are fabricated gradually, yet definitely.

CHAPTER 8:

Bridling the General rule that good energy attracts good

The pattern of good following good expresses that you can draw in good or pessimistic encounters into your life through your viewpoints and sentiments.

Here are a few ways to make the pattern of good following good work for you,

1. Center around inspiration Develop good contemplations and sentiments, as these draw in certain encounters into your life.

2. **Envision your objectives** Shut your eyes and envision yourself encountering the things you need throughout everyday life. See the subtleties and make it genuine to you.

226

3. Be thankful Offer thanks for what you have and for what you need to draw in into your life.

4. Make a move While perception and positive reasoning are significant, you likewise need to make a move towards your objectives.

5. Relinquish opposition Pessimistic considerations and sentiments can hinder the pattern of energy attracting similar energy, so work on relinquishing obstruction and develop an inspirational perspective.

6. Trust the universe-Have confidence that the universe will bring you what you need and let go of connection to the result.

7. Encircle yourself with positive individuals Continuously encircling yourself with individuals who support and empower you can assist you with drawing in certain encounters into your life.

These means are difficult!

In the event that you can rehearse these means consistency that implies you can turn into a fruitful individual extremely quick.

The pattern of good following good is an integral asset that can assist you with bringing positive encounters into your life. By zeroing in on energy, picturing your objectives, offering thanks, making a move, relinquishing opposition, confiding in the universe, and encircling yourself with positive individuals, you can outfit the force of the pattern of good following good and change your life. With these tips, you can make a positive and satisfying life for yourself.

Understanding and Applying the Pattern of good following good

Figuring out how to utilize the pattern of good following good is tied in with getting laser-zeroed in on what you truly need - and encircling yourself with positive energy that will return to you ten times.

1. Recognize YOUR Restricting Convictions

Convictions are things you are sure about, whether about yourself, others or the world. Restricting convictions are the narratives we tell ourselves: "I've forever been bashful" or "I won't ever figure out how to adore turning out." They come from previous encounters and outcomes, your present situation, and the data you've gathered over time. They likewise influence each part of your life. Distinguishing them is the initial step to changing your story and dominating how to involve the pattern of good following good as a manual for accomplishing what you need.

2. Rework YOUR STORY

Everything we say to ourselves is what we accept. As Tony reminds us, "We will act reliably with our perspective on who we genuinely are, regardless of whether that view is precise." Changing your self-talk is fundamental for addressing the inquiry, how does the pattern of good following good work? It is additionally one of the hardest pieces of your pattern of good following good excursion. To draw in energy, you should not just talk and act ostensibly such that shows your objectives. The general rule that good energy attracts good beginnings inside: You should stop negative examples and really have confidence in yourself.

3. SHIFT YOUR Concentration

As Tony frequently says, "Where center goes, energy streams." Don't zero in on disappointments - center around the illustration you learned. Try not to zero in on your past - center around every one of the possible your future holds. In particular, center around your next huge achievement. You are accountable for your feelings and your choices. What do you need most? What provides you motivation and craving? Put all of your energy toward that a certain something and let the pattern of good following good get to work.

4. Make Solid Propensities

Making sound propensities is vital to progress, regardless of whether utilizing the general rule that good energy attracts good. As Tony reminds us, "The contrast between maximized execution and horrible showing isn't knowledge or capacity; most frequently it's the express that your brain and body are in." Yet how might you ensure your body and psyche work in top state? You can begin with objective perception, contemplation and appreciation - three acts of profoundly effective individuals. Picturing your objectives for 10 minutes every morning sets a positive and engaging tone for your day. Contemplation can expand your care and assist you with tracking down your middle and center your considerations. Furthermore, rehearsing appreciation assists you with living at the time and emanate inspiration.

5. Encircle YOURSELF WITH Progress

The primary response to the question, "What is the pattern of good following good?" is this. The strength of the good-following-good pattern depends on your partner. The idea of mirror neurons backs up this idea, however fruitful individuals have known it for a really long time. Tony will tell you that proximity is the source of power. To have an uncommon life, encircle yourself with individuals who improve you."

Escape your impasse work, uneven connections and negative kinships. Raise your principles. Find a guide or a genius bunch so you can impart thoughts to other aggressive individuals. Go to classes and studios with other people who maintain that should improve, be better and make the existence of their fantasies. That energy is infectious - as is achievement.

Instances OF Circumstances Utilizing THE Pattern of good following good

When asking, "What is the good-following-good pattern?" the vast majority consider close connections. They're correct that showing sentiment and enthusiasm is one of the most widely recognized utilizations of the pattern of energy attracting similar energy, yet it is just a single piece of the riddle.

You can utilize this idea to make a forward leap in numerous parts of your life. Need to show a truly amazing job, make the body you need, transform a disappointment into progress or significantly impact your outlook and stop negative reasoning? Figuring out how to utilize the pattern of energy attracting similar energy will assist you with accomplishing these objectives and that's only the tip of the iceberg.

A Caring RELATIONSHIP

Is it true or not that you are caught in that frame of mind of relationship roulette? Do your connections get going with extreme energy and sentiment, just to detonate in a sensational style? Or on the other hand maybe you wind up in average associations that failure after the initial not many months or weeks, leaving you asking why you just really can't find "the one."

It's not difficult to fault your accomplice or conditions when love is subtle, however it at last returns to you. Is it safe to say that you are utilizing the pattern of energy attracting similar energy to show the relationship you really care about? Do you feel you merit a great relationship or do you feel where it counts that nobody will at any point cherish you? Could it be said that you will be defenseless or do you deter yourself from profound close to home associations? Do you deal with finding an accomplice like a shopping list or would you say you are showing genuine romance? While figuring out how to utilize the general rule that good energy attracts good accurately, you should pose yourself these inquiries.

Wellbeing AND Wellness

Like undesirable connections, unfortunate ways of life can feel like an interminable cycle. You shed pounds for a brief time, however consistently set it back on. You begin working out, however you loath it and your new schedules don't stand the test of time. You realize you really want to eat better, however you don't feel you have the self control to oppose the sugar that your body has become used to.

Utilizing the pattern of good following good to make a better way of life starts with your outlook. Turn out to be more aware of your body and notice that solid propensities give you energy and imperativeness. Work on your certainty so you feel more roused to work out. Use objective perception and see yourself succeeding - then get out there and get it going.

Satisfying Vocation

Assuming you feel caught in an unfulfilling vocation, you're in good company. Such countless individuals burn through their experience with occupations they're not enthusiastic about, it nearly appears to be ordinary. You have a steady employment that gives a degree of conviction to your life - why screw with that? This is the specific sort of reasoning that is keeping you from bridling the force of fascination for your vocation.

You can show a satisfying profession or even beginning your own organization - for however long you're willing to work for it. Confront your feeling of dread toward disappointment and foster a profound, relentless faith in yourself. Quit tolerating short of what you merit and increase your expectations. At the point when you put stock in yourself and move toward existence with a good mentality, you'll draw in other people who feel the same way. This is a perfect representation of how the pattern of good following good works.

At the point when you figure out how to utilize the models referenced in this pattern of good following good aide, you will begin to see upgrades in all aspects of your life. You will reap many rewards for the things you put out into the world.

Adjusting Your Contemplations to Monetary Achievement

Adjusting monetary objectives to business targets is vital for the achievement and development of any association. At the point when monetary objectives and business goals are adjusted, it makes a reasonable guide for the association to accomplish its objectives and desires. This article will investigate the significance of adjusting monetary objectives to business targets, the most common way of characterizing business goals and deciding monetary objectives, and different methodologies and best practices to guarantee that monetary objectives are really lined up with business targets.

I might want to see the word 'business visionary' knocked off its platform. Being 'pioneering' is something I search for in organizers to put resources into, yet in addition workers to enlist.

The Significance of Adjusting Monetary Objectives to Business Goals

Adjusting monetary objectives to business targets is fundamental since it guarantees that the monetary assets of an association are used such that backings and drives the accomplishment of its more extensive objectives. At the point when monetary objectives are lined up with business goals, it helps in:

1. Giving lucidity and concentration: By adjusting monetary objectives to business goals, associations can plainly characterize their needs and assign assets likewise. This assists in staying away from wastage of assets on exercises that with doing not add to the general targets of the association.

2. Driving responsibility: When monetary objectives are lined up with business targets, it becomes more straightforward to screen and quantify the advancement towards accomplishing those goals. This makes a feeling of responsibility among the workers and partners, as they know about the monetary targets they need to accomplish to help the association's more extensive objectives.

3. Boosting benefit: Adjusting monetary objectives to business goals empowers associations to recognize and focus on exercises that are probably going to add to productivity. It assists in distributing assets to regions that with having the capacity to create the best yield on venture, subsequently expanding productivity.

4. Working with independent direction: When monetary objectives are lined up with business targets, it gives a structure to settling on educated and vital choices. By taking into account the monetary ramifications of different choices, associations can settle on choices that are in accordance with their drawn out targets and monetary objectives.

5. guaranteeing long haul manageability: When monetary objectives are lined up with business goals, it helps in guaranteeing the drawn out supportability of the association. By zeroing in on monetary objectives that help the development and productivity of the business, associations can make a strong starting point for maintainable achievement.

Characterizing Your Business Goals

Prior to adjusting monetary objectives to business goals, it is vital to characterize the business targets obviously. Characterizing business goals includes recognizing the ideal results and focuses on that the association means to accomplish. Here are a moves toward consider while characterizing your business goals:

1. direct a SWOT investigation: Play out a complete examination of your association's assets, shortcomings, open doors, and dangers. This will help in distinguishing the regions where your association needs to improve and the open doors it can take advantage of.

2. Put forth Brilliant objectives: Guarantee that your business targets are explicit, quantifiable, reachable, significant, and time-bound. Brilliant objectives give lucidity and concentration, making it simpler to adjust monetary objectives to business targets.

3. Include key partners: Counsel and include key partners, including senior administration, division heads, and workers, during the time spent characterizing business goals. This will help in acquiring purchase in and support for the targets and increment the possibilities of effective execution.

4. Focus on goals: Distinguish the main targets that will greatestly affect the progress of your association. Focusing on targets will help in apportioning assets and deciding monetary objectives that are lined up with the most basic goals.

5. Convey goals: Obviously impart the characterized business targets to all partners.

This will guarantee that everybody knows about the objectives and can pursue adjusting monetary objectives to business goals.

Deciding Monetary Objectives for Your Business

When the business targets are characterized, the subsequent stage is to decide monetary objectives that help those goals. Deciding monetary objectives includes setting explicit targets and benchmarks that should be accomplished to help the general goals of the association. Here are a moves toward consider while deciding monetary objectives for your business:

1. Survey authentic monetary information: Investigate the verifiable monetary information of your association to distinguish patterns, examples, and regions that need improvement. This will give bits of knowledge into the monetary exhibition of the association and help in laying out reasonable monetary objectives.

2. Think about outer variables: Consider outside factors that might influence the monetary presentation of your association. This could incorporate economic situations, industry patterns, administrative changes, and cutthroat scene. Understanding these outer elements will help in laying out monetary objectives that are reasonable and feasible.

3. Set quantitative targets: Decide explicit quantitative focuses on that should be accomplished to help the business goals. These objectives could incorporate income development, overall revenues, profit from venture, income, and other monetary measurements that are pertinent to your association.

4. Think about subjective objectives: notwithstanding quantitative targets, consider subjective objectives that are lined up with your business goals. These could incorporate consumer loyalty, representative commitment, brand notoriety, and other non-monetary objectives that add to the general progress of your association.

5. Set reasonable timetables: Lay out sensible courses of events for accomplishing the monetary objectives. Consider the assets accessible, economic situations, and the intricacy of the objectives while setting timetables. Setting practical timetables will help in guaranteeing that the monetary objectives are reachable and can be really lined up with the business goals.

6. Screen progress: Consistently screen and track the advancement towards accomplishing the monetary objectives. This will empower you to distinguish any deviations and make remedial moves if necessary. Checking progress will assist in guaranteeing that the monetary objectives with staying lined up with the business goals and that the association remains focused towards accomplishing its objectives.

Recognizing Key Execution Pointers

key execution markers (KPIs) are quantifiable measurements that assistance in estimating the advancement towards accomplishing the monetary objectives. Recognizing the right KPIs is critical for successfully adjusting monetary objectives to business targets. Here are a moves toward consider while distinguishing key execution markers:

1. Adjust KPIs to business goals: Guarantee that the KPIs are straightforwardly connected to the business targets. This will help in estimating the advancement towards accomplishing those targets and deciding if the monetary objectives are overall successfully lined up with the more extensive objectives of the association.

2. Focus on KPIs: Distinguish the main KPIs that are basic for estimating the monetary exhibition of your association. This could incorporate income development, net revenues, income, profit from speculation, client procurement costs, client lifetime esteem, and other monetary and non-monetary measurements that are pertinent to your business goals.

3. Set focuses for KPIs: Decide explicit targets or benchmarks that should be accomplished for each KPI. These objectives ought to be lined up with the monetary objectives and the more extensive business goals. Setting targets will help in estimating the advancement and deciding if the monetary objectives are by and large actually lined up with the business goals.

4. Utilize a decent scorecard approach: Consider utilizing a fair scorecard way to deal with recognize KPIs. A reasonable scorecard approach considers monetary, client, inner interaction, and learning and development viewpoints. This gives a comprehensive perspective on the association's presentation and assists in adjusting monetary objectives to business goals across various regions.

5. Consistently survey and update KPIs: Survey and update the KPIs consistently to guarantee their pertinence and adequacy. As the business targets and monetary objectives advance, it could be important to change or add new KPIs to quantify the advancement and arrangement precisely.

Making a Financial plan that Supports Your Targets

A financial plan is a monetary arrangement that frames the assessed incomes and costs for a particular period. Making a spending plan that upholds your targets is critical to adjusting monetary objectives to business goals. Here are a moves toward consider while making a spending plan:

1. Assemble monetary information: Gather and break down verifiable monetary information to comprehend the income and cost examples of your association. This will give experiences into the monetary assets accessible and help in setting reasonable financial plan targets.

2. Focus on costs: Distinguish the costs that are basic for accomplishing the business goals. Focus on costs that straightforwardly add to income age, productivity, and the general progress of your association. This will help in assigning assets successfully and guaranteeing that the financial plan upholds the targets.

3. Assign assets: Distribute assets in view of the focused on costs and the monetary objectives. Think about the income projections, cost structure, and the normal profit from speculation while distributing assets. This will help in guaranteeing that the spending plan upholds the goals and that the monetary assets are used in the best and effective way.

4. Incorporate possibility holds: Put away possibility stores to manage startling costs or income setbacks. Counting possibility saves in the spending plan helps in overseeing monetary dangers and guarantees that the association can answer unanticipated conditions without compromising the accomplishment of the goals.

5. Screen and control costs: Routinely screen and control costs to guarantee that they are in accordance with the financial plan. Execute frameworks and cycles to really track and control costs. This will help in guaranteeing that the spending plan stays lined up with the goals and that the monetary assets are used ideally.

6. Survey and reexamine the financial plan: Audit the financial plan consistently and change it if vital. As the business targets and monetary objectives advance, it very well might be important to adjust the financial plan to guarantee its arrangement with the changing requirements of the association.

Systems for Expanding Income and Benefit

expanding income and productivity is a vital target for most associations. By executing compelling systems, associations can adjust their monetary objectives to the target of expanding income and benefit. Here are some processes to think about:

1. Recognize learning experiences: Distinguish valuable learning experiences that are lined up with your business goals. This could incorporate investigating new business sectors, presenting new items or administrations, extending the client base, or differentiating the income sources. By distinguishing learning experiences, associations can define monetary objectives that help the target of expanding income and productivity.

2. Improve estimating systems: Survey and enhance your evaluating procedures to expand income and productivity. Consider factors, for example, market interest, serious scene, cost construction, and client inclinations while setting costs. By carrying out compelling valuing procedures, associations can accomplish their monetary objectives and adjust them to the target of expanding income and productivity.

3. Work on functional effectiveness: Improve functional proficiency to diminish expenses and increment benefit. Recognize regions where cycles can be smoothed out, assets can be used all the more successfully, and waste can be limited. By working on functional productivity, associations can accomplish their monetary objectives and backing the goal of expanding income and benefit.

4. Put resources into showcasing and deals: Put resources into promoting and deals exercises to produce leads, draw in clients, and increment income. Foster designated advertising efforts, influence advanced channels, and give deals preparing to your group to upgrade the viability of your showcasing and deals endeavors. By putting resources into advertising and deals, associations can adjust their monetary objectives to the goal of expanding income and benefit.

5. upgrade client maintenance and fulfillment: Spotlight on improving client maintenance and fulfillment to expand income and productivity. Execute client dedication programs, give superb client assistance, and look for criticism to recognize regions for development. By upgrading client maintenance and fulfillment, associations can accomplish their monetary objectives and adjust them to the target of expanding income and productivity.

6. Investigate vital associations: Investigate key organizations and coordinated efforts to grow your client base, access new business sectors, or influence corresponding assets. By producing vital associations, associations can accomplish their monetary objectives and backing the target of expanding income and productivity.

7. Influence innovation and advancement: Embrace innovation and development to further develop processes, foster new items or administrations, and gain an upper hand. Put resources into innovation foundation, empower a culture of development, and remain refreshed with the most recent patterns and headways in your industry. By utilizing innovation and development, associations can adjust their monetary objectives to the goal of expanding income and productivity.

By executing these procedures, associations can really adjust their monetary objectives to the target of expanding income and productivity. It is vital to persistently screen and assess the viability of these procedures and make changes on a case by case basis to guarantee the accomplishment of monetary objectives.

Overseeing and Alleviating Monetary Dangers

Monetary dangers are intrinsic in any business, and overseeing and moderating these dangers is urgent for adjusting monetary objectives to business targets. Here are a moves toward consider while overseeing and moderating monetary dangers:

1. Recognize and evaluate chances: Distinguish and survey the monetary dangers that your association might confront. This could incorporate market gambles, credit chances, liquidity gambles, functional dangers, and administrative dangers. By distinguishing and

evaluating chances, associations can foster methodologies and measures to alleviate the effect of these dangers on the monetary objectives and business goals.

2. foster gamble the executives methodologies: Foster gamble the board procedures to oversee and moderate the distinguished dangers really. This could incorporate carrying out risk relief measures, differentiating income sources, laying out monetary controls and administration cycles, and creating emergency courses of action. By creating risk the board techniques, associations can adjust their monetary objectives to the goal of relieving monetary dangers.

3. Carry out inner controls: serious areas of strength for execute controls to guarantee the precision, unwavering quality, and trustworthiness of monetary data. This incorporates laying out strategies and methodology, isolating obligations, directing customary interior reviews, and executing powerful monetary revealing frameworks. By executing inward controls, associations can adjust their monetary objectives to the target of guaranteeing the monetary strength and honesty of the association.

4. Screen and audit risk the board measures: Consistently screen and survey the adequacy of the gamble the executives measures. This incorporates leading gamble appraisals, following key gamble markers, and assessing the effect of chance moderation methodologies. By checking and surveying risk the board measures, associations can adjust their monetary objectives to the target of successfully overseeing and alleviating monetary dangers.

5. Remain refreshed with administrative necessities: Remain refreshed with the advancing administrative prerequisites and guarantee consistence with pertinent regulations and guidelines. This remembers checking changes for bookkeeping principles, charge guidelines, and monetary announcing prerequisites. By remaining refreshed with administrative necessities, associations can adjust their monetary objectives to the goal of keeping up with legitimate and administrative consistence.

6. Foster a gamble the board culture: Cultivate a gamble the executives culture inside the association by advancing mindfulness, responsibility, and straightforwardness. This remembers giving preparation and schooling to take a chance with the board, empowering open correspondence about gambles, and perceiving and remunerating risk the executives endeavors. By fostering a gamble the executives culture, associations can adjust their monetary objectives to the goal of installing risk the board into their everyday tasks.

By actually overseeing and alleviating monetary dangers, associations can adjust their monetary objectives to the target of guaranteeing the drawn out monetary solidness and progress of the association.

Observing and Assessing Monetary Execution

Observing and assessing monetary execution is fundamental for adjusting monetary objectives to business goals. By routinely evaluating the monetary presentation, associations can distinguish areas of progress, measure progress towards the monetary objectives, and make restorative moves if necessary. Here are a moves toward consider while observing and assessing monetary execution:

1. Lay out execution measurements: Lay out execution measurements that are lined up with the monetary objectives and business targets. This could incorporate income development, net revenues, profit from speculation, income, and other monetary measurements that are applicable to your association. By laying out execution measurements, associations can quantify the advancement and arrangement of the monetary objectives with the business targets.

2. Foster revealing systems: Foster detailing components to track and report the monetary presentation consistently. This could incorporate fiscal summaries, the board reports, dashboards, and key execution marker (KPI) scorecards. By creating detailing components, associations can screen and assess the monetary exhibition and arrangement with the business targets actually.

3. Lead customary monetary surveys: Direct standard monetary audits to evaluate the monetary exhibition and recognize regions for development. This incorporates breaking down monetary information, contrasting genuine execution and the objectives, and recognizing any deviations. By directing customary monetary surveys, associations can quantify the advancement towards the monetary objectives and make restorative moves if essential.

4. Dissect patterns and examples: Break down patterns and examples in the monetary information to acquire bits of knowledge into the presentation and arrangement of the monetary objectives with the business goals. This incorporates recognizing solid areas, regions for development, and any possible dangers or amazing open doors. By breaking down patterns and examples, associations can pursue educated choices to guarantee the arrangement regarding the monetary objectives with the business targets.

5. Look for outer input: Look for outside criticism from monetary specialists, advisors, or industry companions to acquire an objective point of view on the monetary execution. This can give significant bits of knowledge and proposals to working on the arrangement of the monetary objectives with the business targets. By looking for outside criticism, associations can get a more extensive perspective on their monetary presentation and distinguish regions for development.

6. Make restorative moves: Make remedial moves on the off chance that any deviations are recognized during the checking and assessment process. This could incorporate updating monetary objectives, redistributing assets, carrying out new systems, or adjusting existing cycles. By making restorative moves, associations can guarantee that the monetary objectives are actually lined up with the business goals and that the association keeps focused towards accomplishing its objectives.

By observing and assessing monetary execution, associations can quantify the advancement towards the monetary objectives, recognize regions for development, and guarantee the arrangement of the monetary objectives with the business targets.

Changing Monetary Objectives on a case by case basis

Changing monetary objectives depending on the situation is essential to guarantee their arrangement with the changing necessities of the association. As the business climate develops, associations might have to change their monetary objectives to answer new open doors or difficulties. Here are a few variables to consider while changing monetary objectives:

1. Survey the business targets: Consistently audit the business goals to guarantee their significance and arrangement with the association's vision and mission. Assuming that the business targets transform, it could be important to change the monetary objectives likewise to help the new goals.

2. Screen the outside climate: Screen the outer climate for any progressions that might influence the monetary objectives. This could remember changes for economic situations, client inclinations, administrative necessities, or cutthroat scene. By remaining mindful of the outer climate, associations can change their monetary objectives to answer the progressions successfully.

3. Evaluate the interior abilities: Survey the inner capacities and assets of the association to decide whether they are lined up with the monetary objectives. In the event that the association comes up short on important assets or capacities to accomplish the monetary objectives, it very well might be important to change the objectives in like manner or put resources into fostering the expected assets.

4. Look for criticism from partners: Look for input from key partners, including representatives, clients, providers, and financial backers, on the monetary objectives and their arrangement with the business goals. This can give important experiences and points of view that might require changes in accordance with the monetary objectives.

5. Assess the monetary exhibition: Consistently assess the monetary presentation and measure the advancement towards the monetary objectives. In the event that the association isn't on target to accomplish the objectives, it very well might be important to change the objectives or foster new methodologies to guarantee their achievement.

6. Think about long haul maintainability: Consider the drawn out supportability of the association while changing monetary objectives. Finding some kind of harmony between momentary monetary targets and the drawn out monetary soundness and development of the organization is significant.

By changing monetary objectives depending on the situation, associations can guarantee their arrangement with the changing requirements of the association and increment the possibilities accomplishing the general goals.

Praising and Remunerating Monetary Achievement

Commending and remunerating monetary achievement is significant for inspiring workers, perceiving accomplishments, and supporting the arrangement of monetary objectives with business targets. Here are a few methodologies for commending and compensating monetary achievement:

1. Lay out execution based motivating forces:
Lay out execution based motivators that are straightforwardly connected to the accomplishment of the monetary objectives and business targets. This could incorporate rewards, benefit sharing projects, or investment opportunities that reward workers for their commitments to the monetary progress of the association.

2. Perceive and value accomplishments:
Perceive and value the accomplishments of people and groups who have added to the monetary achievement. This should be possible through open acknowledgment, grants, declarations, or different types of appreciation. By perceiving accomplishments, associations can support the arrangement of monetary objectives with business goals and persuade representatives to proceed with their endeavors.

3. share examples of overcoming adversity: Offer examples of overcoming adversity and contextual investigations that feature the monetary accomplishments and their arrangement with the business targets. This should be possible through interior interchanges, bulletins, or other correspondence channels. By sharing examples of overcoming adversity, associations can move and inspire workers and build up the significance of adjusting monetary objectives to business targets.

4. Praise achievements and targets: Commend the accomplishment of achievements and focuses on that add to the monetary achievement. This could incorporate getting sorted out extraordinary occasions, group excursions, or different festivals to recognize the advancement and achievement. By praising achievements and targets, associations can establish a positive and spurring workplace that energizes the arrangement of monetary objectives with business goals.

5. Support peer acknowledgment: Energize peer acknowledgment by engaging workers to appreciate and perceive each other's commitments to the monetary achievement. This should be possible through shared acknowledgment programs, input channels, or group gatherings. By empowering peer acknowledgment, associations can encourage a culture of coordinated effort and shared help, which improves the arrangement of monetary objectives with business targets.

6. Give proficient improvement potential open doors: Give proficient improvement open doors to representatives as a prize for their commitments to the monetary achievement. This could incorporate financing preparing programs, supporting certificates, or giving chances to professional success. By giving proficient advancement open doors, associations can show their obligation to representative development and improvement, which reinforces the arrangement of monetary objectives with business targets.

By praising and compensating monetary achievement, associations can propel workers, perceive accomplishments, and support the arrangement of monetary objectives with business targets.

All in all, adjusting monetary objectives to business goals is significant for the achievement and development of any association. By following the means and methodologies illustrated in this article, associations can really adjust their monetary objectives to their more extensive business targets. From characterizing business targets and deciding monetary objectives to overseeing monetary dangers and observing monetary execution, each step assumes a crucial part in guaranteeing the arrangement and accomplishment of monetary objectives. By putting resources into the right assets, encouraging cooperation and correspondence across divisions, and praising and compensating monetary achievement, associations can make a culture that upholds the arrangement of monetary objectives with business targets.

CHAPTER 9:

Mind-Body Association with Monetary Prosperity

Clinicians realize that the survival switch in our mind was at first required for those brushes with death that early people frequently confronted. Regardless of present day conditions being moderately "safe," stress can in any case enact this survival desire, and it frequently leaves us intellectually depleted and depleted. Regardless of being a worry for quite a long time, it is just lately that emotional wellness has earned respect as a subject meriting conversation, goal and even appreciation.

We presently view dealing with our brains as like how we fuel the cells and muscles in our bodies — realizing it can prompt long haul benefits. Notwithstanding, as a nation captivated with a high speed, continuously working, objective situated way of life, I'm here to bring up that on the off chance that you're not dealing with your psychological well-being, numerous parts of your life will begin to decline — including your funds. It doesn't make any difference how much cash you are making, in the long run, these unfortunate behavior patterns can find your ledger.

Monetary Pressure And Monetary Health

Emotional wellness and monetary prosperity are two significant parts of our lives that are in many cases seen in confinement from one another. Nonetheless, truly these two components are profoundly entwined and assume a significant part in deciding our general wellbeing and bliss.

The Connection Between Monetary Pressure And Psychological wellness

Stress is a major danger to both our psychological well-being and monetary prosperity. In view of its risky nature, stress mists our judgment and prompts rash choices that can have harming results on our funds. Settling on great monetary choices is more earnestly when our psychological well-being is tested, as you may be more inclined to motivation buys, not taking care of bills on time or not saving sufficient cash to develop your investment account. These activities, thus, just compound the monetary pressure we experience.

The actual costs of pressure, like sleep deprivation and weariness, further compound the issue. On top of this, the present financial environment heaps on an extra layer of pressure that can essentially influence our emotional wellness. Battles to meet costs, save for the future or even earn a living wage can bring out sensations of uneasiness and wretchedness. Toss in an unstable fluctuating business sector where you can watch your retirement reserve funds balance sway all over, and the pressure can make even the most prepared financial backer carry on of dread.

The Significance Of Taking care of oneself In Monetary Prosperity

Taking care of oneself is critical to both mental and monetary prosperity. At the point when we deal with our physical and emotional wellness, we can pursue better monetary choices and deal with our funds with more prominent certainty. Taking care of oneself exercises, for example, exercise, contemplation and side interests can assist us with lessening pressure, work on our concentration and keep up with our psychological and close to home equilibrium.

You might consider how you can have a solid relationship with cash when each move you make for your wellbeing and prosperity accompanies a sticker price, yet putting resources into your psychological well-being doesn't need to burn through every last dollar. Here are only a couple of minimal expense or free tips you can use to start decreasing the monetary pressure in your life:

• **Planning And Arranging:** A financial plan tracker and arranging application can assist you with effectively checking your ways of managing money and ensure you are remaining affordable for you. This will permit you to see precisely where your cash is proceeding to make any fundamental acclimations to guarantee you save enough and abstain from overspending.

• **Computerize Your Funds:** By setting up programmed moves for bills and reserve funds, you will not need to stress over dealing with various installments and can be sure that your bills will be paid on time and your reserve funds will keep on developing.

• **Set Customary Monetary Audits:** It is enticing to need to check your retirement accounts day to day, yet fixating on day to day market variances might cause more damage than great.

• **Versatile Treatment:** Portable restorative administrations can be a practical method for

273

tending to any emotional wellness concerns, both monetarily related and in any case. With these sorts of administrations, you approach a specialist from anyplace, permitting you to all the more likely deal with your feelings of anxiety while in a hurry.

• **Meet With A Monetary Expert:** While this could have all the earmarks of being the costliest on this rundown, over the long haul, working with a monetary expert will assist with diminishing the everyday and deep rooted burdens that accompany dealing with your funds. They can assist you with making a spending plan, put forth monetary objectives and proposition guidance on the most proficient method to properly deal with your cash. By having an expert aide you, you can feel sure about your monetary choices and lessen pressure connected with cash the board.

It's memorable's vital that emotional well-being and monetary prosperity remain closely connected and disregarding one will at last effect the other. Whether you're battling with monetary pressure or just hoping to work on your general wellbeing, find opportunity to put resources into both and focus on your prosperity.

All encompassing Ways to deal with Abundance

At the point when we hear the expression "creating financial stability," it's not difficult to relate it exclusively with the amassing of cash and resources. While monetary security and flourishing are fundamental parts of abundance, genuine abundance includes considerably more than just dollars and pennies. The SUPERCHARGED® excursion to monetary achievement accentuates the significance of information, energy, effect, and objective setting so you can live with more euphoria and reason.

Construct a Well off Library of Information: Put resources into Yourself

Perhaps of the most significant resource you can procure on your way to creating financial momentum is information. Training, in the entirety of its structures, can be an integral asset for individual and monetary development. This is the way you can construct a rich library of information:

Ceaseless Learning: Growing long term financial stability starts with an inquisitive psyche. Focus on deep rooted realizing, whether through proper instruction, self-study, or mentorship. Keep awake to-date with the most recent advancements in your field and investigate new areas of premium.

Monetary Education: To go with informed monetary choices, you should grasp the standards of cash the executives, effective financial planning, and planning. Carve out opportunity to work on your monetary proficiency through books, courses, and online assets.

Self-improvement: Creating financial stability isn't just about gathering cash; it's additionally about self-improvement. Put resources into personal growth through books on self-improvement, care, and initiative.

Organizing: Our Manager Sovereign, Kwanza Jones generally says, "Nobody succeeds alone… once in a while you want a lift." It's essential to encircle yourself with individuals who can share their insight and encounters. Systems administration can give important bits of knowledge and amazing open doors that you wouldn't view as all alone. Also, being around similar individuals is propelling; their achievements can motivate new objectives for you to seek after. It's not difficult to arrive at your objectives all alone, however it's such a ton more straightforward when you have a local area that you can rest on for help, similar to the

Follow Your Energy: The Force of Making every moment count

Monetary achievement is a shared objective, it shouldn't come to the detriment of your satisfaction and satisfaction. Chasing after your energy is an indispensable part of creating financial momentum, as it can prompt both monetary achievement and individual fulfillment. The following are four moves toward assist you with accomplishing this:

Recognize Your Enthusiasm: Find opportunity to find what really energizes you. What are your inclinations, side interests, and abilities? Distinguishing your energy will drive your desire and responsibility.

Transform Energy into Pay: Whenever you've distinguished your enthusiasm, investigate how you can adapt it. This could include beginning a side business, chasing after a lifelong in a connected field, or offering administrations or items that are lined up with your inclinations.

Perseverance: Creating financial momentum through your energy might take time and exertion. Remain committed, even notwithstanding difficulties and misfortunes.

Diligence is much of the time the way to transforming energy into benefit.

Work-Life Joining: While at the same time seeking after your energy, remember the significance of work-life combination. Ponder exercises that will keep you roused and help your prosperity rate. Break these exercises into more modest activities and coordinate them into your day to day everyday practice. These activities will become propensities that will assist you with arriving at your objectives without significant penances. It's feasible to create financial wellbeing while at the same time partaking in a satisfying individual life.

Coordinating Physical and Monetary Wellbeing

Pursuing a fulfilled and prosperous life, the blend of physical and money related prosperity emerges as a fundamental rule. These two perspectives, regularly found in separation, are erratically associated, influencing each other in habits that loosen up past straightforward

279

numbers on a scale or in a record. This comprehensive method for managing flourishing sees the agreeable association among physical and money related prosperity, pushing for a good and intentional lifestyle that develops as a rule.

Sorting out the Interconnectedness: The Physical-Money related Nexus

The nexus among physical and money related prosperity is laid out in the affirmation that the success of one viewpoint generally impacts the other. For example, real prosperity directly influences one's ability to work, secure compensation, and seek after sound money related decisions. Simultaneously, money related tension and fragility can show really, impacting in everyday prosperity and criticalness. Understanding this interconnectedness lays the groundwork for an exhaustive method for managing thriving.

The Impact of Real Prosperity on Financial Success

Real Wellbeing and Calling Proficiency

Real wellbeing isn't simply a groundwork of thriving yet moreover a driver of calling proficiency. Individuals in extraordinary real prosperity often experience higher energy levels, further created obsession, and worked on mental clearness. These characteristics add to extended work capability and ampleness, finally influencing proficient achievement and pay improvement.

Clinical consideration Costs and Money related Security

Staying aware of genuine prosperity expects an imperative part in easing clinical benefits costs, a basic money related thought. Individuals who center around preventive clinical benefits through normal movement, changed sustenance, and wellbeing practices are every now and again less leaned to consistent disorders. Accordingly, they are better arranged to administer clinical expenses, shielding financial consistent quality long term.

Protection Installments and Genuine Success

The state of genuine prosperity clearly impacts protection installments. Individuals in ideal prosperity much of the time fit the bill for lower life and medical care charges, provoking conceivable cost hold reserves. This money related benefit fills in as an inspiration for taking on a proactive method for managing genuine flourishing, as it directly impacts the monetary piece of security.

Proficiency and Money related Benefit

Focuses dependably show a positive association between's genuine work and extended productivity. Whether through standard work-out plans, care practices, or an accentuation on adequate rest, individuals who center around their genuine success regularly experience elevated mental ability and imagination. These characteristics convert into additional created work execution, conceivably inciting money related rewards, for instance, headways and remuneration increases.

The Effect of Money related Prosperity on Genuine Success

Induction to Clinical consideration and Wellbeing Resources

Money related prosperity basically impacts a particular's induction to clinical benefits and wellbeing resources. Adequate money related resources consider standard prosperity check-ups, preventive screenings, and permission to quality clinical consideration organizations. Then again, financial objectives could confine one's ability to place assets into preventive measures, conceivably inciting clinical issues that could have been tended to proactively.

Stress and Its Physiological Effects

283

Money related pressure is a typical variable with direct physiological outcomes. Consistent money related concerns can add to raised sensations of uneasiness, inciting conditions, for instance, hypertension, a resting problem, and compromised resistant capacity. Keeping an eye on financial concerns and taking on sound money related rehearses are basic pushes toward progressing mental and genuine success.

Food and Financial Choices

Money related resources accept a fundamental part in trim dietary choices. Individuals with stable financial conditions could deal with the expense of a fair and nutritious eating schedule, adding to ideal genuine prosperity. Of course, money related objectives could provoke reliance on more affordable, less nutritious food decisions, conceivably influencing in everyday prosperity and success.

Real Environment and Money related Constancy

Financial robustness influences everyday conditions, which, in this manner, impact real prosperity. Individuals with financial means can pick conditions that help flourishing, including induction to green spaces, wearing workplaces, and a safeguarded region. Conflicting with the standard, financial hardships could achieve ordinary conditions that add to tension and mull over prosperity.

Balance among fun and serious exercises and Autonomy from a futile daily existence

Money related prosperity is interlaced with the ability to achieve a pleasant harmony among serious and fun exercises. Individuals with a sound financial foundation could have the flexibility to zero in on confidential flourishing, including adequate rest, entertainment activities, and quality time with loved ones. Discovering some sort of concordance among work and individual life is a basic piece of all things considered and profound prosperity.

Procedures for Integrating Physical and Financial Prosperity

Complete Preparation: Zeroing in on Prosperity Utilization

Thorough arranging incorporates assigning resources not only to financial responsibilities yet furthermore to prosperity related utilizes. This integrates making arrangements for practice focus enlistments, prosperity tasks, and preventive clinical consideration measures. By survey prosperity as a non-easy to refute adventure, individuals can develop a proactive method for managing genuine flourishing.

Financial Instruction for Prosperity Hypotheses

Financial training connects past standard dares to integrate prosperity related financial decisions. Getting a handle on the money related repercussions of prosperity choices, security consideration, and clinical benefits plans draws in individuals to seek after informed decisions that line up with both their physical and financial targets.

Supervisor Wellbeing Ventures: Using Corporate Assistance

Various organizations offer prosperity programs as an element of their delegate benefits. These drives much of the time consolidate health inspirations, close to home prosperity resources, and preventive clinical consideration measures. Agents can utilize these ventures to work on their genuine thriving while potentially reducing clinical benefits costs, adding to both physical and financial prosperity.

Hold assets for Prosperity Emergencies: Making a Security Net

Money related orchestrating should integrate game plans for prosperity emergencies. Spreading out a hidden bonanza unequivocally doled out for clinical benefits costs ensures that astounding clinical costs don't mull over's money related robustness. This security net gives internal sensation of congruity and supports the relationship between financial sensibility and genuine flourishing.

Placing assets into Preventive Clinical benefits: Long stretch Money related benefit

Zeroing in on preventive clinical benefits measures, for instance, ordinary check-ups, screenings, and a strong lifestyle, is a proactive interest in long stretch money related benefit. The cost of preventive thought is regularly out and out lower than the expenses related with treating progressing afflictions that could rise out of disregarding genuine prosperity.

Changing Lifestyle Development: Cautious Spending Choices

As money related conditions improve, individuals could experience lifestyle development — a penchant to increase getting a charge out of with rising compensation. Cautious spending choices ensure that extended financial technique add to a sensible and sound lifestyle, recollecting utilizations for health, prosperity works out, and invigorating sustenance.

Financial Expecting Profound wellbeing: Past Genuine Success

Money related prosperity loosens up to mental success. Coordinating profound prosperity considerations into financial organizing incorporates anticipating treatment, coordinating, or wellbeing practices that help up close and personal and mental thriving. This exhaustive technique sees the confusing relationship between mental, physical, and financial prosperity.

Changing Financial Goals to Prosperity Targets

Spreading out financial goals that line up with prosperity targets concocts a firm framework for the most part flourishing. Whether setting something to the side for health equipment, making plans for a prosperity retreat, or making arrangements for quality banquets, changing money related targets to prosperity desires develops the interconnected thought of physical and financial prosperity.

The Occupation of Attitude in Far reaching Flourishing

Flood Mindset: Developing Prospering in All Perspectives

Fostering a flood demeanor transcends financial advantage to integrate all components of thriving. This viewpoint perceives the interconnectedness of physical and money related prosperity, developing a demeanor of appreciation for the resources that add to a prosperous and fulfilling life.

Positive Affinities: The Foundation of Far reaching Achievement

Coordinating positive inclinations into ordinary timetables shapes the basis of far reaching achievement. Whether in financial practices, for instance, arranging and saving or genuine penchants like standard action and a nice eating routine, positive timetables add to upheld flourishing across the two perspectives.

Self-Reflection and Goal Setting: A Complete Procedure

Ordinary self-reflection and goal setting are vital for a far reaching method for managing flourishing. Individuals can review their physical and financial targets, perceive districts for improvement, and put forth deliberate objectives that line up with their vision of a prosperous and strong life.

Appreciation Deals with: Supporting Satisfaction

291

Practicing appreciation is a valuable resource for supporting fulfillment in both physical and money related spaces. Perceiving the good pieces of prosperity and financial success empowers a sensation of fulfillment, supporting the widely inclusive nature of flourishing.

Troubles and Strategies for Overcoming Obstacles

Time Restrictions: Powerful Joining

Time restrictions regularly present challenges to consolidating physical and financial prosperity practices. Viable joining incorporates recognizing proficient frameworks, for instance, coordinating genuine work into everyday timetables or uniting financial readiness with care practices. Streamlining tries ensures that the two perspectives get thought without overwhelming plans.

Conflicting Necessities: Troublesome activity

Conflicting necessities could arise, especially when brief money related stresses battle with long stretch genuine prosperity targets. Discovering some sort of amicability remembers centering for exercises that address the two perspectives simultaneously, for instance, embracing wise prosperity rehearses and chasing after financial decisions that line up with prosperity targets.

External Strains: Strength and Cutoff points

External strains, whether social suppositions or workplace demands, can affect choices associated with physical and money related prosperity. Making strength and characterizing limits are key procedures for investigating external strains, ensuring that decisions line up with individual thriving rather than outside presumptions.

Developing Circumstances: Flexible Procedures

Life is dynamic, and changing circumstances could require adaptable procedures. Whether facing money related setbacks or experiencing shifts in genuine prosperity, individuals can foster flexibility by embracing change and meaningfully altering their ways of managing line up with current circumstances.

A Journey Towards Thorough Flourishing

Planning physical and financial prosperity is definitely not a goal yet a relentless journey towards sweeping flourishing. It incorporates seeing the complex dance between these two viewpoints, sorting out their agreeable relationship, and embracing purposeful practices that add to success in all pieces of life. As individuals set out on this journey, may it lead to a huge sensation of balance, fulfillment, and overcoming prospering that encompasses both the physical and money related spaces.

CHAPTER 10:

Supporting Your Cash Magnet Mentality

In the area of individual bookkeeping and overflow creation, the power of mindset could never be more huge. A money magnet standpoint transcends basic financial penchants; it wraps a huge change in discernment that attracts flood and flourishing. Supporting this viewpoint is a momentous outing that incorporates creating positive convictions, embracing financial strength, and taking on deliberate practices that line up with the principles of overflow interest.

Sorting out the Money Magnet Demeanor: The Foundation of Achievement

The money magnet attitude is grounded in the conviction that one's examinations and viewpoints towards cash influence financial outcomes. It underscores the meaning of developing a positive mental structure that is focused on overflow notwithstanding customary monetary education. At its middle, the money magnet viewpoint perceives the interconnectedness of examinations, sentiments, and financial genuine elements.

The Principles of a Money Magnet Mindset

1. Flood Mindfulness: Moving from Lack to Abundance

Flood comprehension is the groundwork of a money magnet viewpoint. It incorporates moving from a lack outlook, which bases on hindrances and need, to a mindset of abundance that sees the vast open doors for overflow creation. Embracing flood clears the path for viable fixes, open entryways, and a standpoint that attracts flourishing.

2. Positive Insight: Showing Money related Goals

Positive portrayal is a preparation that incorporates obviously imagining and experiencing one's money related goals. By making mental pictures of achievement, flood, and money related achievements, individuals program their mind cerebrums to agree with these positive outcomes. Discernment fills in as a vital resource for showing desires and supporting the confidence in the achievability of money related targets.

3. Rehearsing Appreciation: Empowering Fulfillment and Fascination

Appreciation is a noteworthy power that upholds fulfillment and attracts sure energy. Creating appreciation practices, such as keeping an appreciation journal or conveying thanks reliably, changes individuals to the flood in their lives. A grateful heart transforms into a magnet for extra gifts, making a positive analysis circle that upholds the money magnet mindset.

4. Financial Adaptability: Investigating Troubles with Excellence

Financial adaptability is the ability to investigate troubles and mishaps with ease and confirmation. Taking on a money magnet mindset incorporates considering impediments to be any entryways for improvement, learning, and refinement. Individuals with flexibility can recuperate from monetary mishaps, keep an uplifting perspective, and reaffirm their confidence in their ability to defeat snags.

5. Discerning Spending: Adjusting Costs to Individual Qualities Cognizant spending is the act of adjusting consumptions to one's own needs and values. A money magnet standpoint loosens up past gathering overflow to coming to deliberate conclusions about how money is spent. By placing assets into experiences, things, and organizations that influence one's characteristics, individuals make a pleasing association between their financial affinities and their general life goals.

6. Center around Cooperation: Utilizing Aggregate Energy Joint effort and aggregate success are embraced by a cash magnet mentality. Seeing that flood is positively not a lose circumstance, individuals with this mindset really search for important entryways for facilitated exertion, sorting out, and generally beneficial associations. A helpful standpoint utilize total energy, making a synergistic influence that heightens the appealing draw of wealth.

Supporting the Money Magnet Mentality: A Weighty Trip
Legitimate Affinities for Overflow Insight

1. Assertions for the Afternoon: Programming the Mind Cerebrum

Ordinary accreditations are minimized, positive clarifications that individuals repeat to themselves regularly. These assertions build up sure convictions about overflow and abundance by reinventing the psyche mind. By dependably affirming decrees, for instance, "I'm a money magnet" or "Flood streams to me effectively," individuals embed these convictions into their brain, developing a persevering through cash magnet viewpoint.

2. Discernment Services: Reviving Targets

Discernment services incorporate saving committed time for obviously imagining and experiencing money related targets. This preparing goes past direct gazing vacantly at nothing in particular; it's a purposeful and focused mental movement. Vision sheets, directed symbolism meetings, or vivid mental excursions in which individuals see, feel, and experience the accomplishment of their monetary objectives are instances of representation customs.

3. Appreciation Journaling: Fostering a Flood Disposition

Keeping an appreciation journal is a practical and effective inclination for supporting the money magnet viewpoint. Consistently, individuals record things they are appreciative for, including financial blessings, likely entryways, and positive experiences. This preparing fosters a flood standpoint by redirecting thought from deficiency towards the swarm inspirations to be thankful, making a foundation for upheld overflow discernment.

4. Progress and Instruction: Progressing with Money related Knowledge

A money magnet viewpoint embraces interminable learning and personal development. Individuals who like to keep as such of reasoning effectively search for monetary instruction, read books about bringing in cash, and keep awake to date on speculation open doors. This commitment to learning isn't just about accumulating data anyway about creating with financial understanding, changing methods, and developing's cognizance one could decipher overflow.

5. Care Works on: Being Accessible with Assets

Care practices incorporate being totally present and conscious in the continuous second. Applied to reserves, care infers checking approaches to overseeing cash, chasing after deliberate financial decisions, and fostering a sensation of control over cash matters. By making major areas of strength for a between one's activities and one's monetary expectations, care rehearses like careful spending and planning add to continuous abundance cognizance.

6. Legislative strategy in regards to minorities in the public eye: Making a move With Reason A positive mentality isn't just about thinking decidedly; it furthermore remembers administrative strategy in regards to minorities for society. The people who keep up with this mentality find purposeful ways to arrive at their monetary goals. This could involve laying out achievable monetary achievements, creating plans that can be done, and reliably making progress toward these objectives. Administrative arrangement with respect to minorities in the public arena develops the conviction that conscious undertakings lead to unquestionable results, further supporting the money magnet viewpoint.

Supporting Flexibility in Financial Hardships

1. Reconsidering Challenges: Seeing Entryways in Mishaps

Strength is vital to supporting the money magnet attitude, especially notwithstanding financial troubles. Rather than survey incidents as troublesome checks, individuals with this mindset reconsider hardships as any entryways for advancement and learning. This mental shift engages them to keep an elevating point of view

303

and push toward challenges with a response arranged attitude.

2. Flexibility: Versatility in Financial Systems

Financial scenes are dynamic, and supporting the money magnet demeanor requires adaptability. Individuals zeroed in on this viewpoint understand the meaning of being versatile in money related frameworks. This could incorporate changing hypothesis portfolios, exploring new income sources, or turning money related plans considering developing circumstances. Adaptability ensures that troubles don't wreck the overall bearing towards overflow mindfulness.

3. Financial Planning: Building a Flexible Foundation

Financial organizing is a fundamental gadget for supporting adaptability. Individuals with a money magnet mindset take part in exhaustive financial organizing that consolidates emergency holds, risk the board, and substitute strategies. A completely inspected financial game plan fills in as serious areas of strength for a, giving a manual for investigating hardships while staying agreed with long stretch money related goals.

4. Neighborhood: Supporting Total Strength

A consistent neighborhood significant in supporting strength during money related challenges. Individuals with a money magnet mindset really search for and support networks where experiences can be shared, encounters exchanged, and support publicized. Total strength transforms into areas of strength for a, developing the conviction that troubles are brief and that a neighborhood comparable individuals can add to beating money related hindrances.

5. Cautious Reflection: Eliminating Models from Troubles

Cautious reflection is a preparation that incorporates purposely checking out and

305

eliminating models from financial disasters. As opposed to pestering dissatisfaction, individuals with a money magnet standpoint use setbacks as any entryways for self-revelation and improvement. Considering hardships energizes an improvement standpoint, supporting the conviction that incidents are fundamental bits of the journey towards upheld overflow comprehension.

Balancing Overflow Mindfulness with Sensibility

1. Financial Obligation: Counterbalancing Dreams with this present reality

While supporting a money magnet mindset incorporates clearing thinking, it is crucial to counterbalance dreams with financial responsibility. Individuals support overflow awareness by laying out their desires in sensible money related decisions. This integrates sensible preparation, really looking at costs, and ensuring that financial targets line up with current circumstances while allowing space for advancement.

2. Spreading out Viable Goals: Noticing Progressive Triumphs

Supporting the money magnet disposition requires spreading out reasonable and doable financial targets. Celebrating consistent successes, paying little heed to how little, develops the conviction that progress is being made. Sensible goal setting develops conviction and motivation, adding to an upheld sensation of reinforcing and overflow comprehension.

3. Hypothesis Insight: Development and Resistance

Adventure decisions expect a crucial part in supporting overflow perception. Individuals with this standpoint embrace adventure understanding that consolidates development, tirelessness, and a long perspective. Expanding adventures mitigates risks, and steadiness thinks about the escalating effect on spread out over an extended time. These guidelines add to a viable method for managing overflow creation.

4.Financial Cutoff points: Balancing Lifestyle with Hold reserves

Staying aware of financial cutoff points is vital for supporting overflow mindfulness. While individuals with this disposition esteem the fulfillment all through daily existence, they furthermore spread out cutoff points to ensure that lifestyle choices line up with long stretch money related targets. This congruity between participating in the present and making plans for what the future holds adds to a pragmatic and fulfilling overflow comprehension.

5. Taking on Sound Financial Inclinations: Routine and Consistency

Supporting overflow mindfulness incorporates embracing strong money related penchants as a component of one's day to day practice. This could integrate standard spending plan reviews, solid venture finances responsibilities, and irregular assessments of money related goals. By coordinating these affinities into everyday presence, individuals develop the relationship between their exercises and the widely inclusive norms of overflow interest.

Overcoming Ordinary Hardships in Supporting Overflow Mindfulness

1. Outside Effects: Investigating Social Pressures

Outside influences, as social presumptions and social norms, can introduce challenges to supporting overflow comprehension. Individuals could face strain to change in accordance with materialistic standards or appreciate lifestyle development. Vanquishing these incites incorporates staying steady with individual characteristics, characterizing limits, and contradicting outside pressures that conflict with the principles of a money magnet mindset.

2. Assessment Trap: Focusing in on Individual Journey

The assessment trap, often filled by electronic diversion and external benchmarks, can undermine overflow mindfulness. Individuals supporting this standpoint see that everyone's financial outing is exceptional. Rather than standing out themselves from others, they base on their solitary progression, commending achievements and acquiring from challenges without being impacted by external benchmarks.

3. Irritability and Second Fulfillment: Creating Perseverance

Irritability and a hankering for second joy are ordinary challenges in supporting overflow comprehension. Overcoming these tendencies incorporates creating perseverance and understanding that overflow creation is a consistent cooperation. Individuals zeroed in on this demeanor see the value of conceded fulfillment and embrace the trip, accepting that anticipated undertakings will yield persevering through results.

4. Sensation of fear toward Disillusionment: Embracing Improvement Attitude

The sensation of fear toward frustration can forestall upheld overflow mindfulness. Individuals with a money magnet mindset embrace an advancement standpoint, considering dissatisfactions to be any entryways for learning and improvement. Rather than being weakened by fear, they approach troubles with adaptability, interest, and a conviction that disasters are brief steps while heading to persevering through progress.

5. Balancing Present Delight with Future Planning

Balancing present delight with future organizing is a constant test in supporting overflow discernment. Individuals investigate this balance by taking on a cautious method for managing lifestyle choices, ensuring that ongoing joys line up with long stretch money related goals. This harmony appreciates life while keeping a limited and conscious method for managing overflow creation.

A Durable Journey of Overflow Perception

Supporting a money magnet mindset is certainly not a goal; it's a well established journey of creating perception, deliberate exercises, and tenacious turn of events. It incorporates supporting positive convictions, acclimating to challenges with adaptability, and planning overflow perception into the surface of everyday presence. As individuals set out on this momentous journey, may they find that supporting a money magnet mindset attracts financial flood as well as energizes a critical sensation of fulfillment, reason, and persisting through flourishing.

Day to day Practices for Long haul Flourishing

Pursuing long stretch achievement, the power of everyday practices can't be underestimated. These practices, when dependably woven into the surface of everyday presence, might conceivably shape one's money related heading, develop an overflow aware mindset, and lay out the foundation for getting past flourishing. From cautious money related penchants to intentional goal setting, this examination dives into the unprecedented impact of everyday practices on the outing towards upheld wealth.

The Importance of Ordinary Practices in Laying out serious areas of strength for an establishment

The best approach to financial prospering is definitely not a run at this point a significant distance race, requiring consistent effort and intentional choices. Everyday practices go about

313

as the construction impedes that shape the bearing of this trip. By integrating cautious inclinations, fostering an uplifting perspective, and changing exercises to long stretch financial goals, individuals can show themselves a way towards upheld wealth. This examination plunges into the multifaceted pieces of regular chips away at, offering pieces of information into how they add to the overall goal of long stretch achievement.

Cautious Financial Inclinations: Supporting a Sound Association with Money

1. Arranging with Reason: A Framework for Money related Accomplishment

Arranging is the underpinning of sound money related organization. Regular arranging practices incorporate following compensation, expenses, and save assets with an explanation driven standpoint. By making a sensible spending plan that lines up with financial targets, individuals gain an indisputable understanding of their money related scene and can seek after informed decisions to achieve long stretch thriving.

2. Splendid Spending: Making Informed Money related Choices Everyday

Keen spending is a regular practice that remembers making due with intentional and informed choices about utilizes. By surveying needs versus needs, searching for an impetus for cash, and avoiding drive purchases, individuals can foster a penchant for cautious spending. This preparing adds to extended save reserves, diminished money related pressure, and the protecting of resources for long stretch laying out areas of strength for an establishment.

3. Automated Hold reserves: Consistency in Building Financial Stores

Electronic speculation reserves is areas of strength for a to day practice that ensures consistency in building money related stores. By setting up customized moves to hold assets or adventure accounts, individuals center around saving without the necessity for consistent manual intervention. This preparing imbues money related discipline, makes a security net for emergencies, and spreads out a foundation for long stretch overflow assortment.

4. Commitment The board: Taking care of Commitment Bit by bit

Regular commitment the board practices incorporate tracking down a way consistent ways of taking care of wonderful commitments. This could integrate making unsurprising portions, zeroing in on over the top interest commitments, and searching for open entryways for commitment decline. By watching out for commitment purposely reliably, individuals get ready for autonomy from a futile way of life and unrestricted laying out monetary steadiness astounding entryways.

5. Money related Tutoring: Everyday Learning for Informed Route

Zeroing in on ordinary money related preparing is a preparation that empowers individuals to go with informed decisions about their money. Whether through scrutinizing financial composition, following reliable money related news sources, or partaking in electronic courses, predictable learning works on money related training. Informed route transforms into a penchant, adding to a more secure and prosperous financial future.

Fostering an Overflow Aware Viewpoint: Molding Thoughts for Flood

1. Ordinary Declarations: Programming the Mind Cerebrum

Everyday accreditations are an extraordinary gadget for trim an overflow discerning viewpoint. By admitting positive clarifications associated with flood, thriving, and financial accomplishment, individuals program their mind minds for positive convictions. This everyday practice develops a standpoint that attracts

317

wealth and positions individuals to benefit by important entryways for long stretch flourishing.

2. Portrayal Functions: Envisioning Financial Accomplishment Everyday

Portrayal functions incorporate everyday gatherings of particularly imagining and experiencing financial accomplishment. By making mental pictures of achieved goals, individuals develop their confidence in the plausibility of thriving. Portrayal practices go past certain thinking; they interface with the inventive psyche to foster a significant sensation of sureness and supposition for long stretch money related flood.

3. Appreciation Journaling: Empowering Joy and Fascination

Keeping an appreciation journal is an ordinary practice that supports fulfillment and attracts sure energy. By regularly seeing down things to be thankful for, including money related leans toward and astounding entryways, individuals support a flood standpoint. Appreciation journaling makes a good info circle that adds to an upheld sensation of joy and an overflow mindful perspective.

4. Care in Money related Course: Staying Present

Care practices contact financial bearing, including staying present and totally took part in the event. By monitoring financial choices, avoiding hurried decisions, and considering long stretch results, individuals foster an inclination for cautious money related living. This regular practice develops the relationship among exercises and the overall norms of overflow mindfulness.

5. Positive Relationship with Money: Changing Convictions Everyday

Changing feelings about cash is a nonstop everyday practice that incorporates testing and reshaping confining convictions. By purposely interfacing cash with positive credits, similar to an open door, open entryways, and the ability to have a productive result, individuals shift their standpoint towards review overflow as an instrument for making a delightful and prosperous life.

Intentional Goal Setting: Everyday Strides Towards Long stretch Accomplishment

1. Spreading out Sensible Everyday Targets: Noticing Continuous Victories

Everyday goal setting incorporates isolating greater money related focuses into commonsense and doable everyday targets. By setting centers for hold reserves, commitment lessening, or adventure responsibilities, individuals celebrate continuous wins everyday. This preparing builds up momentum, helps assurance, and develops the conviction that consistent undertakings lead to long stretch accomplishment.

2. Evaluating and Evolving Targets: Flexibility in Journey for Thriving

Reliably investigating and changing money related targets is an ordinary practice that ensures course of action with creating conditions. Individuals who participate in this preparing stay versatile and adaptable, making informed acclimations to their targets considering advancing necessities, money related scenes, and life changing circumstances. This flexibility adds to upheld progress towards long stretch achievement.

3. Ordinary Movement Plans: Changing Targets into Significant Advances

Everyday movement plans incorporate isolating money related targets into undeniable, huge stages. By making an everyday aide for achieving express objectives, individuals make a translation of desires into practical exercises. This regular practice gives clearness as well as works with the dependable execution of endeavors that add to long stretch money related accomplishment.

4. Following Headway: A Regular Assessment of Money related Outing

Following headway is an everyday practice that incorporates assessing money related movements, noticing accomplishments, and taking into account achievements. By reliably researching financial standing and perceiving progress, individuals stay motivated and gain significant pieces of information into their trip towards long stretch thriving. This preparing supports an awareness of certain expectations and commitment to financial targets.

5. Noticing Regular Achievements: Fostering a Rousing point of view

Celebrating regular achievements, paying little heed to how little, is a preparation that fosters a motivational viewpoint on the financial outing. By perceiving and recognizing triumphs, individuals support the conviction that their undertakings are making a difference. This elevating input adds to a viewpoint of progress, strength, and the supposition for continued with prospering.

Counterbalancing Present Joy with Future Readiness: A Friendly Procedure

1. Cautious Spending Choices: Agreeing with Long stretch Goals

Cautious spending choices incorporate ordinary decisions that line up with both present delight and long stretch financial targets. By deliberately picking utilizations that add to by and large flourishing and line up with individual characteristics, individuals discover some sort of congruity between participating in the present and making plans for a prosperous future. This preparing ensures that ordinary choices support the general target of long stretch achievement.

2. Everyday Hold subsidizes Responsibilities: Making Consistent Monetary security

Regular save subsidizes responsibilities, paying little mind to how subtle, add to steady laying out monetary steadiness. By making a penchant for saving a piece of pay ordinary, individuals make a consistent instance of saving. This preparing assembles money related stores as well as supports the discipline of saving, a critical part in long stretch flourishing.

3. Routine Money related Enlistments: Staying aware of Financial Care

Routine money related enlistments incorporate everyday assessments of financial trades, account changes, and progress towards targets. By remaining really attracted with money related issues, individuals keep a raised level of financial care. This everyday practice ensures that any deviations from the organized money related course can be quickly tended to, adding to the overall security of long stretch flourishing.

4. Balance in Lifestyle Choices: Regular Reflection on Needs

Changing lifestyle choices is a regular practice that incorporates contemplating necessities and reaching conscious decisions about utilizations. By reliably evaluating the plan of lifestyle choices with long stretch financial targets, individuals ensure that their regular exercises add to a neighborly and sensible method for managing flourishing.

5. Standard Money related Readiness: An Everyday Commitment to Advance

Standard financial orchestrating is a regular commitment to advance that incorporates examining, changing, and making arrangements for what the future holds. By committing time consistently to financial planning, individuals really add to the trim of their money related destiny. This preparing ensures that regular exercises line up with a completely inspected plan for long stretch achievement.

Investigating Challenges: Developing Fortitude for Upheld Prospering

1. Cautious Powerful in Hardships: A Regular Practice

Cautious choice creation during challenges is an ordinary practice that incorporates pushing toward hindrances with a peaceful and deliberate viewpoint. By avoiding impulsive reactions and then again making informed choices, individuals investigate challenges with flexibility. This everyday practice develops the conviction that troubles are brief and reasonable steps on the journey towards upheld achievement.

2. Flexibility: Versatility in Everyday Financial Frameworks

Adaptability is a regular practice that perceives the influential thought of financial scenes. By remaining versatile in ordinary money related systems, individuals adjust to developing circumstances, make the most of possibilities, and rout challenges. This preparing ensures that the mission for long stretch prospering is portrayed by strength and adaptability.

3. Money related Strength Practices: Regular Steps Towards Sufficiency

Everyday financial flexibility practices incorporate intentional exercises to manufacture areas of strength for a. This could consolidate adding to emergency holds, extending hypotheses, or searching for capable guidance. By coordinating these practices into everyday timetables, individuals support their financial strength and prepare for unexpected continues while heading to long stretch prospering.

4. Neighborhood: Ordinary Responsibility for Total Strength

Attracting areas of strength for with is an everyday practice that adds to total adaptability. By sharing experiences, searching for direction, and offering support, individuals manufacture an association that develops adaptability during

327

testing times. This ordinary practice develops the perception that a neighborhood comparative individuals can add to beating financial obstacles and supporting long stretch thriving.

5. Cautious Reflection on Challenges: Everyday Learning for Advancement

Cautious reflection on challenges is an everyday practice that incorporates isolating representations from incidents. By deliberately thinking about inconveniences and acquiring from them, individuals change troubles into astonishing entryways for improvement. This ordinary practice empowers an improvement standpoint, developing the conviction that disasters are essential bits of the outing towards upheld prospering.

A Well established Commitment to Prospering Through Regular Practices

Pursuing long stretch flourishing, ordinary practices emerge as the key part that interfaces desires with this present reality. Creating cautious money related penchants, forming an overflow perceptive standpoint, spreading out intentional targets, counterbalancing present bliss with future planning, and investigating hardships with adaptability — this enormous number of ordinary practices add to a developing further monetary establishment adventure that transcends transient triumphs. As individuals center around incorporating these practices into their customary schedules, may they track down that the road to upheld thriving isn't simply reachable yet furthermore improving, empowering, and altogether pivotal.

Advancing Your Outlook as You Develop Monetarily

The journey towards financial improvement isn't just about gathering wealth; a phenomenal odyssey incorporates propelling one's viewpoint to agree with newfound money related genuine elements. As individuals progress on their money related journey, from starting financial security to extended overflow, the psychological scene goes through tremendous changes. This examination plunges into the complicated exchange between financial turn of events and attitude headway, offering pieces of information into the psychological developments, challenges, and entryways that go with the ascending to more noticeable flourishing.

The Strong Relationship Among Assets and Viewpoint Headway

Setting out on the method of money related improvement is a dynamic and complex endeavor that goes past the space of monetary trades. As individuals experience an extension in money related success, their viewpoint goes through an equivalent turn of events, framing perceptions, viewpoints, and feelings about wealth. This examination dives into the amicable association between money related improvement and attitude progression, underlining the significance of understanding and investigating the psychological region that goes with the journey towards progress.

1. Spreading out Money related Strength and Security

Standpoint Characteristics: Foundation Building and Security

In the hidden periods of the money related trip, the consideration is on spreading out robustness and security. The mindset is depicted by a sensation of care, a consideration on arranging, and a highlight on building a money related foundation. Individuals center around saving, arranging, and spreading out emergency resources for make an inclination that everything is great and defend against unforeseen financial troubles.

Challenges: Sensation of fear toward Deficiency and Overemphasis on Prosperity

Challenges during this stage much of the time twirl around a sensation of fear toward deficiency. Individuals may be unnecessarily careful, hesitant to continue with painstakingly weighed out game-plans, and may go against hypotheses or experiences that could really yield more imperative returns. Overemphasis on prosperity can confine money related improvement, and overcoming this challenge requires a sensible technique that perceives the meaning of both security and painstakingly weighed out game-plan taking.

Open entryways: Building Financial Discipline and Learning

The starting period of money related dauntlessness gives opportunities to building financial discipline and fostering a learning standpoint. Individuals can focus in on acquiring money related schooling, getting a handle on hypothesis decisions, and cultivating the capacities fundamental for effective money the board. This stage lays the groundwork for future financial improvement by giving major penchants and data.

2. Accelerating Advancement and Growing Compensation

Demeanor Characteristics: Yearning, Expansion, and Laying out monetary steadiness

As individuals experience a speed expansion in money related improvement and an extension in pay, the viewpoint goes through a shift towards want and laying out long haul monetary soundness. The middle reaches out past straightforward unfaltering quality to indispensable overflow gathering. There is an elevated knowledge of entryways, and individuals actually search for streets for extending pay, researching hypotheses, and developing financial portfolios.

Challenges: Changing Craving and Sensible Route

Challenges at this stage could rise out of a staggering longing that can incite rushed bearing. Changing the drive for advancement with sensible route becomes critical. Individuals ought to investigate the motivation to seek after quick gains and well actually embrace a fundamental method for managing laying out monetary security that lines up with long stretch money related targets.

Open entryways: Fundamental Endeavors and Improvement

This stage presents open entryways for fundamental endeavors and portfolio upgrade. Individuals can research an extent of theory decisions, from stocks and land to endeavors, attempting to overhaul returns while regulating bets. Key money related planning and the improvement of an improvement arranged mindset become key for helping open entryways during this stage.

3. Achieving Plushness and Money related Comfort

Mindset Credits: Money related Comfort, Flood, and Lifestyle Choices

As financial wealth is accomplished, the standpoint shifts towards a sensation of money related comfort and flood. Individuals experience a more noticeable degree of chance in making lifestyle choices, and there is an accentuation on participating in the results of money related accomplishment. The mindset embraces a greater perspective on wealth, consolidating monetary points of view as well as lifestyle, experiences, and charitableness.

Challenges: Balancing Enjoyment with Functional Overflow The leaders

Challenges in this stage turn around changing the have a great time money related achievement with efficient overflow the load up. There may be a drive to appreciate excessive going through or method of time on earth extension. Individuals ought to intentionally foster a viewpoint that esteems the value of viable overflow practices, cautious spending, and long stretch money related arrangement.

Likely entryways: Liberality, Legacy Building, and Sweeping Overflow

Achieving extravagance opens ways of opening entryways for philanthropy, legacy building, and the mission for exhaustive overflow. Individuals can really partake in compensating society, make a getting through legacy, and explore streets for mindfulness past financial benefits. This stage offers the chance to consider overflow to be a gadget for constructive outcome and fulfillment.

4. Supporting and Saving Wealth

Demeanor Ascribes: Stewardship, Legacy Shielding, and Money related Knowledge

At the period of supporting and saving overflow, the mindset forms into one of stewardship. There is a significant sense of responsibility towards shielding the gathered overflow for individuals later on. Money related knowledge transforms into a fundamental belief, and individuals successfully search for strategies for legacy preservation, long stretch legitimacy, and the careful organization of their financial legacy.

Challenges: Overflow Preservation amidst Financial Developments and Social characteristics

Challenges at this stage could rise up out of outside financial developments, changes in the financial scene, and the complexities of social quirks. Supporting and shielding overflow requires a sharp perception of money related designs, proactive financial readiness, and strong correspondence inside family structures. Investigating generational overflow move transforms into a key idea.

337

Astounding entryways: Indispensable Endeavors, Continued To learn, and Mentorship

Open entryways for fundamental hypotheses, continued learning, and mentorship present themselves during this stage. Individuals can research creative endeavor procedures, stay informed about progressing money related business areas, and take part in mentorship to confer their gathered knowledge to what's to come. The middle developments towards making a persevering through impact and adding to the financial success of individuals later on.

Investigating Viewpoint Progression: Key Techniques for Improvement and Achievement

1. Consistent Learning and Adaptability

A vow to constant learning is a vital strategy for investigating mindset improvement. As money related scenes advance, staying informed about market designs, hypothesis open entryways, and monetary developments is major. Individuals should foster a flexible disposition that embraces change, headway, and the obtainment of new data.

2. Cautious Reflection and Objective Reassessment

Standard reflection on money related goals and reassessment of one's requirements is crucial at each period of the financial journey. Cautious reflection grants individuals to change their creating disposition to their continuous cravings, changing goals and procedures relying upon the circumstance. This preparing ensures that the mission for overflow stays predictable with individual characteristics and long stretch dreams.

3. Key Money related Arrangement

Key money related orchestrating is a groundwork of investigating mindset improvement. Individuals should take part in comprehensive financial organizing that contemplates present second and long stretch goals, risk opposition, and adventure techniques. This fundamental strategy gives a manual for money related improvement while keeping major areas of strength for an amidst weaknesses.

4. The ability to see the value in anybody on a more profound level in Money related Route

The ability to comprehend individuals on a significant level expects an essential part in investigating viewpoint improvement. Understanding and managing sentiments associated with money related decisions is essential. This consolidates seeing the impact of fear, greed, and various sentiments on free bearing and creating significant adaptability to head with sound money related choices.

5. Neighborhood Mentorship Responsibility

Dynamic responsibility with solid organizations and mentorship associations contributes through and through to viewpoint advancement. Sharing experiences, searching for urging, and acquiring from the understanding of guides make areas of strength for a. These affiliations offer huge pieces of information, various perspectives, and essential consolation during the various periods of the money related journey.

A Far reaching Method for managing Financial and Mental Wealth

Fostering one's mindset as money related improvement happens is an essential piece of a complete method for managing wealth. The journey towards flourishing isn't solely about cash related gains yet incorporates a massive difference in convictions, mindsets, and perspectives. By investigating mindset improvement with deliberateness, consistent learning, and a promise to sweeping wealth, individuals can make a reasonable and fulfilling relationship with their financial trip. May this examination go about as a helper for those on the method of money related advancement, engaging them to embrace the creating scene of both financial and mental wealth.

Conclusion

Unlocking the Treasury Within

As we wandered through the pages of "Change Your Mind Into a Money Magnet," the examination of changing contemplations into financial flood spread out like the launch of a particularly watched store. From the initiation of understanding the impact of positive thinking to jumping into the intricacies of everyday practices that charge wealth, the story has been an aide for those attempting to change their minds major areas of strength for into of progress.

In our main goal to change the mind into a money magnet, we observed that overflow isn't just about unquestionable assets; it's a state of discernment. The power of positive demands, the portrayal functions that laid out particular pictures of financial accomplishment, and the appreciation journaling that instilled our trip

343

with fulfillment were the brushes we used to make a masterpiece of viewpoint change.

We meandered into the fundamental spaces of everyday chips away at, investigating the nuances of cautious financial penchants, intentional goal setting, and the delicate dance of counterbalancing present fulfillment with future planning. Each part was a wandering stone, building the expansion between financial dreams and their undeniable affirmation.

In seeing the challenges and chances of supporting a money magnet mindset, we faced the external effects and internal battles that can prevent our outing. Nonetheless, through flexibility, adaptability, and a guarantee to improvement, we observed that incidents are not bypasses yet rather wandering stones towards persevering through progress.

The segments on creating mindset as money related improvement spreads out were an exhibition of the remarkable exchange between overflow assortment and mental change. We found that the journey towards extravagance isn't immediate yet a development through stages, each mentioning its surprising mindset and presenting its unquestionable hardships and entryways.

As we wrap up this remarkable excursion, review that the cerebrum is a conclusive organizer of your financial destiny. It's not just about social event cash; about fostering a standpoint attracts and upholds wealth. The safe inside your cerebrum is incredible, holding on for you to open its favored bits of knowledge and manifest the financial flood you merit.

May this journey be a catalyst for changing your mind into a ceaseless money magnet — a wellspring of overflow that streams effectively, copiously, and enduringly. As you convey the pieces of information from these pages into your everyday daily practice, may your cerebrum continue to resound with the repeat of prospering, attracting significant entryways, and polarizing overflow in habits past whatever you might at any point envision.

This isn't just the completion of a book; it's the beginning of one more segment in your money related trip. Embrace the change, harness the impact of your cerebrum, and may your life be a showing of the unfathomable potential that spreads out when you change your mind into a real money magnet.

Review page

Dear Reader,

Welcome to the Review Page for "Turn Your Thoughts into Wealth"!

Reviews:

Mind-Blowing Insights!

This book is a game-changer! The author seamlessly combines practical strategies with a touch of inspiration. Each chapter is a gem, revealing secrets to transform your thinking and attract wealth. A must-read for anyone seeking financial abundance and a positive mindset.

Share Your Thoughts:

Have you read "Turn Your Thoughts into Wealth"? We'd love to hear your thoughts and experiences. Drop your review below and join the community of readers on this transformative journey!

Happy Reading,

Jose R. Johnson